JEFF KOONS
AT THE ASHMOLEAN
7 February–9 June 2019

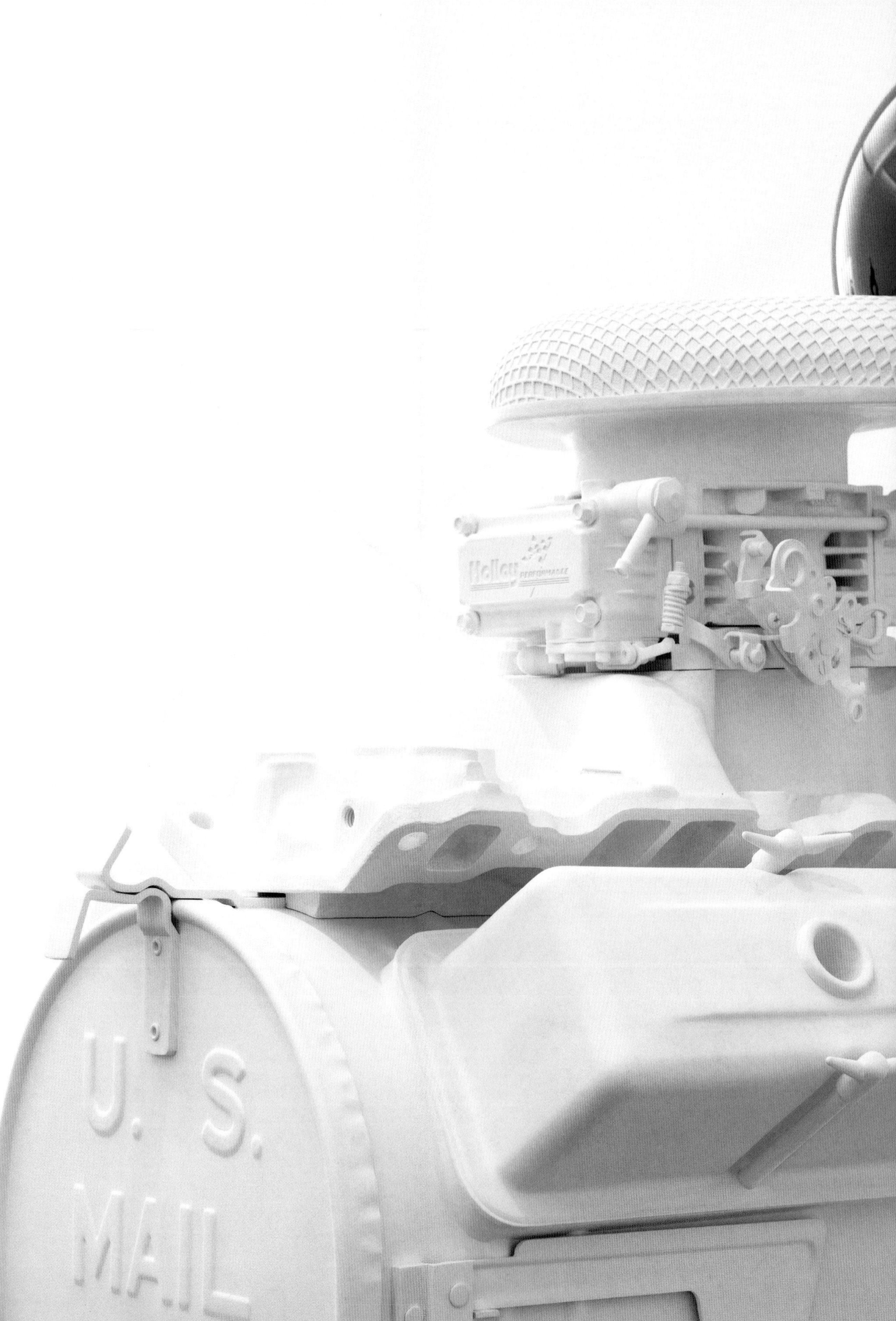
Holley
U.S.
MAIL

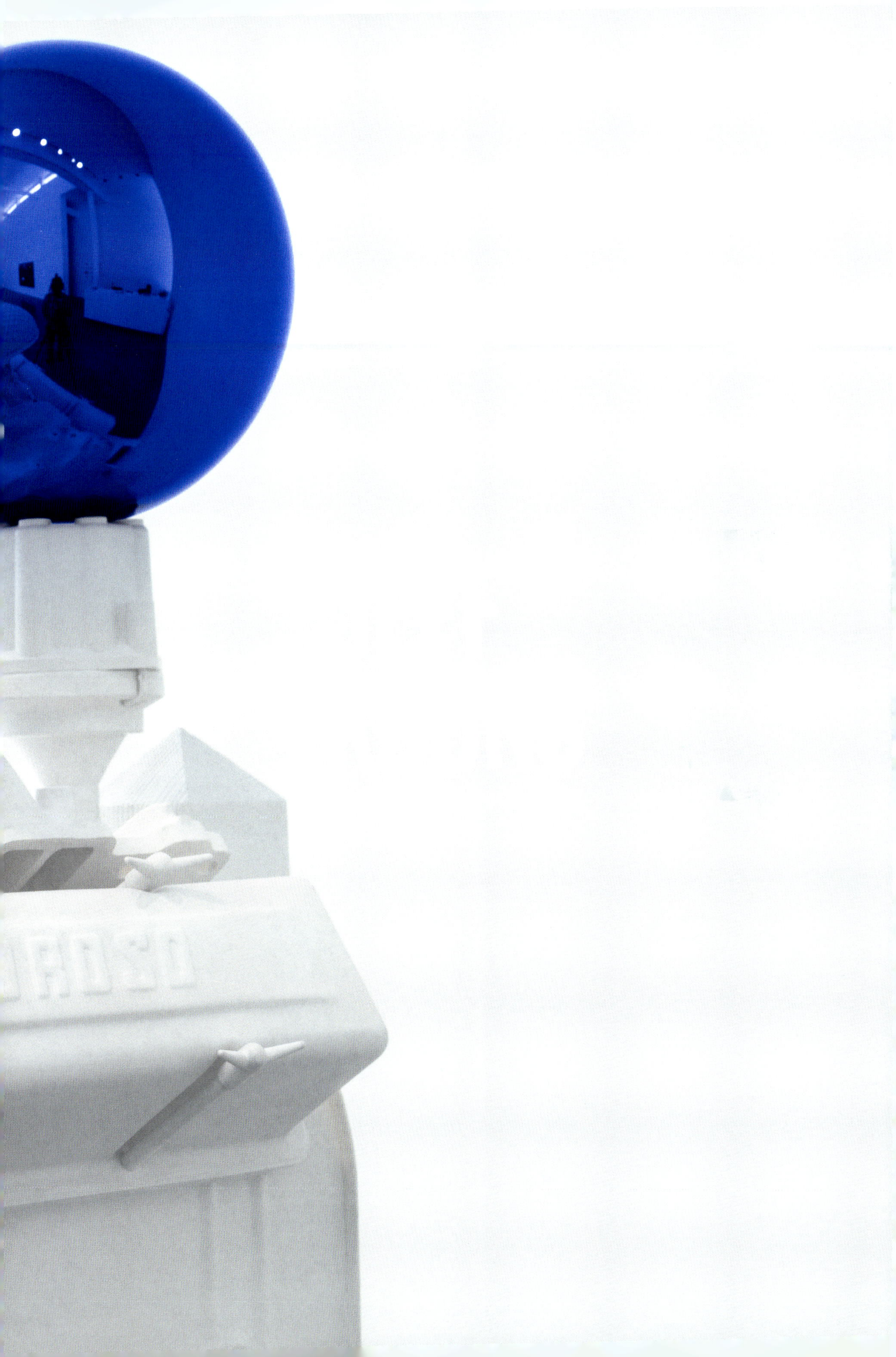

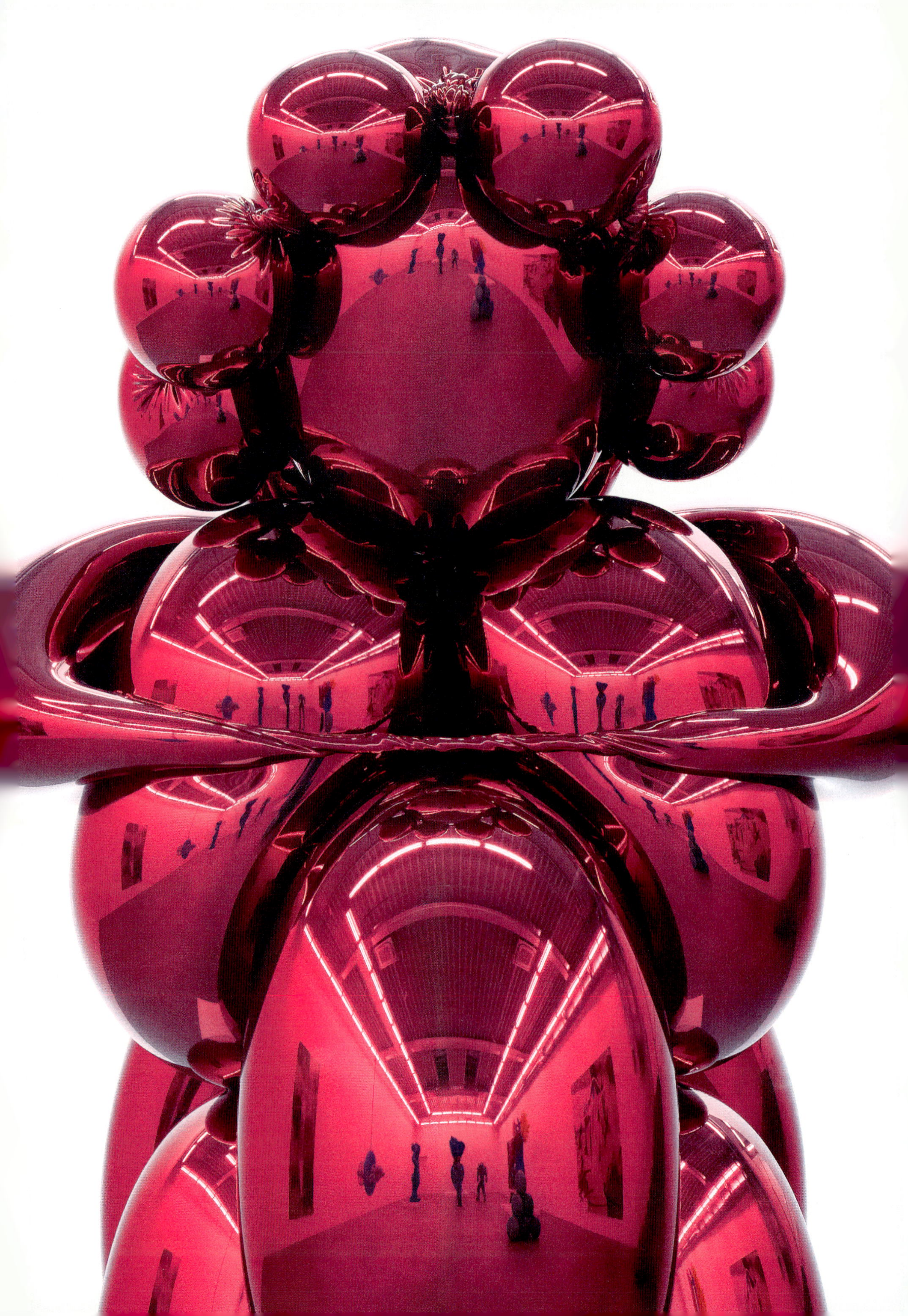

CONTENTS

[opposite]
Detail of *Balloon Venus (Magenta)*, 2008–12
© Jeff Koons. Photo: Marc Domage, Almine Rech Gallery

[previous spread]
Detail of *Gazing Ball (Mailbox)*, 2015
© Jeff Koons. Photo: Fredrik Nilsen, 2017. Courtesy Gagosian

The exhibition has been supported generously by:
Miyoung Lee and Neil Simpkins
Larry Gagosian
Friends of the Ashmolean
and others who wish to remain anonymous

ISBN: 978-1-910807-29-3

British Library Cataloguing in Publication Data.
A catalogue record for this book is available from the British Library.

Designed by Ocky Murray
Printed and bound in Belgium by Albe de Coker

ASHMOLEAN

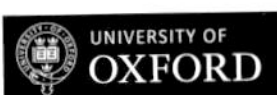

DIRECTOR'S FOREWORD

The Ashmolean's first connection with Jeff Koons took place in 2015 around the exhibition we mounted, in collaboration with the Hall Art Foundation, of the work of Ed Paschke. A Chicago imagist, Paschke was one of Koons's early teachers and played a significant, frequently acknowledged role in his artistic development. Jeff kindly lent four works from his collection to the exhibition and was interviewed by Norman Rosenthal for the catalogue (*Ed Paschke: Visionary from Chicago 1968–2004*, Ashmolean Museum, 2015).

Koons's first visit to the Ashmolean came a little over a year later – at the invitation not of the Museum, but of Oxford's undergraduate art-history society. In 2017 the Edgar Wind Society, named after the first professor of art history at Oxford, inaugurated an award for an 'Outstanding Contribution to Visual Culture'. With the confidence of youth, they decided to present the inaugural award to Jeff Koons and invited him to Oxford to receive it. To the surprise of some, but not to those who are familiar with the artist's consideration and generosity, he flew over for the day to accept the award and talk to the students in the Museum. It seems particularly fitting, given the Ashmolean's distinct role as a university museum, that the seeds for the current exhibition were sown through a student initiative. Later that year Koons returned with his wife and some friends to spend more time in the Museum, and following that we broached the idea of working with him on an exhibition in Oxford focused on his work. This exhibition offered an opportunity to explore the long cultural history represented within the Museum, on which Koons draws and to which he responds. It was an idea to which he enthusiastically agreed.

A visit to Jeff Koons's studio is an intriguing and revealing experience. An anonymous and unprepossessing building in the lower west side of Manhattan, only a small plate bearing the word 'studio' above a doorbell offers any hint to the activity within. The door opens into a clean, white, open-plan office. Here you are welcomed by Gary, Jeff's quietly spoken, genially gnomic but evidently masterful studio manager. Small-scale models of planned exhibitions and gallery layouts sit on tables together with exhibition catalogues and books, their pages bookmarked with yellow 'post-it' notes. On my last visit Jeff greeted me with his distinctly American brand of gracious charm and solicitousness, while sipping coffee from a 'Venus of Willendorf' mug.

The studio has an atmosphere of calm and focused industry. Voices are low while requests from Jeff – for a piece of information, a visual reference or a scale model to place within a gallery model – are swiftly and efficiently answered. Next door in a small room, dominated on one visit by Koons's large, gleaming yellow sculpture of *Pluto and Proserpina*, more people sit at monitors, creating and manipulating 3D computer models and watching parts of as yet unrealised sculptures twist on their screens. Doors lead off into further rooms beyond. Passing a life-size, computer-generated cut-out of a planned steel sculpture of a deer pursued by hounds, you enter the painting studio. Here further quietly industrious assistants work at re-creating some of the masterpieces of Western Art for the *Gazing Ball* painting series. Works by Titian, Rubens and Velazquez apparently line the walls, some of them unnervingly on their side.

The process through which these paintings are produced is astonishingly painstaking, with an attention to detail that tilts towards the obsessive. Once the composition is mapped out with broad tonal underpainting, the painting is divided into small irregular areas (about the size of an A5 sheet) in which the colour is meticulously analysed. In each area several hundred different colours and shades might be identified; these are then mixed in paint and extruded in toothpaste-sized dollops onto a palette. Each colour is then applied in turn through perfectly aligned stencils into which tiny holes have been punched. In short, the picture is created in paint, pixel by pixel, before a further campaign produces a unified whole. After the stencils the paintings are then hand painted, using prints outs of high resolution images of the original painting as reference. Similar degrees of meticulous reconstruction take place in the sculpture gallery next door, where gleaming white casts of ancient sculptures, including the monumental Farnese Hercules, hold court.

What is clear from even a brief studio visit is the degree of authority and artistic control exerted in these processes by Koons himself. Every decision is considered, every tiny variation in finish and appearance explored and agreed at every stage. This control is reflected in, if not embodied by, Koons's work, giving it much of its peculiarly and particularly charged nature. We are clearly in a world far removed from the nineteenth-century artist's garret and its attendant Romantic ideas about the frenzy of solitary artistic creation. But there are equally clearly parallels between Koons's studio and the artist studios of an earlier age, in which a medieval or Renaissance master would be surrounded by innumerable assistants. Each would have his own specialism, from the construction of panels or priming of canvases to the mixing of colours or the painting of foliage or drapery. However, it does remain curious that while this collective process of artistic production is standard practice today in the workshop of an architect or fashion designer, it continues – even now – to excite comment in the visual arts.

This exhibition would not have been possible without the wholehearted and generous collaboration of Jeff Koons himself as well as his studio. I would particularly like to thank Gary McCraw, Diana Matuszak, Lauran Rothstein and Hannah Spitz for all their help with the practical elements of the exhibition and their unflagging support throughout the project. The exhibition took shape and was developed in collaboration with Sir Norman Rosenthal who, in his role as honorary contemporary curator at the Ashmolean, has done so much to support the development of the Museum's contemporary art programme and who has also contributed an essay to this catalogue. No one likes to part with their works by Jeff Koons and so I would also like to thank The Broad Art Foundation, BZ and Michael Schwartz, Stefan T. Edlis and Almine and Bernard Ruiz-Picasso, as well as other private collectors, for their generosity in agreeing to do so. The mounting of such an exhibition is an involved and complicated business and it would not have been possible without the support of others and heartfelt thanks are due to Larry Gagosian, Neil Simpkins and Miyoung Lee, The Friends of the Ashmolean Museum, as well as others who wish to remain anonymous, for their generous help and to Jeff Koons once again for his generosity in producing a limited edition print in support of the exhibition.

Xa Sturgis
December 2018

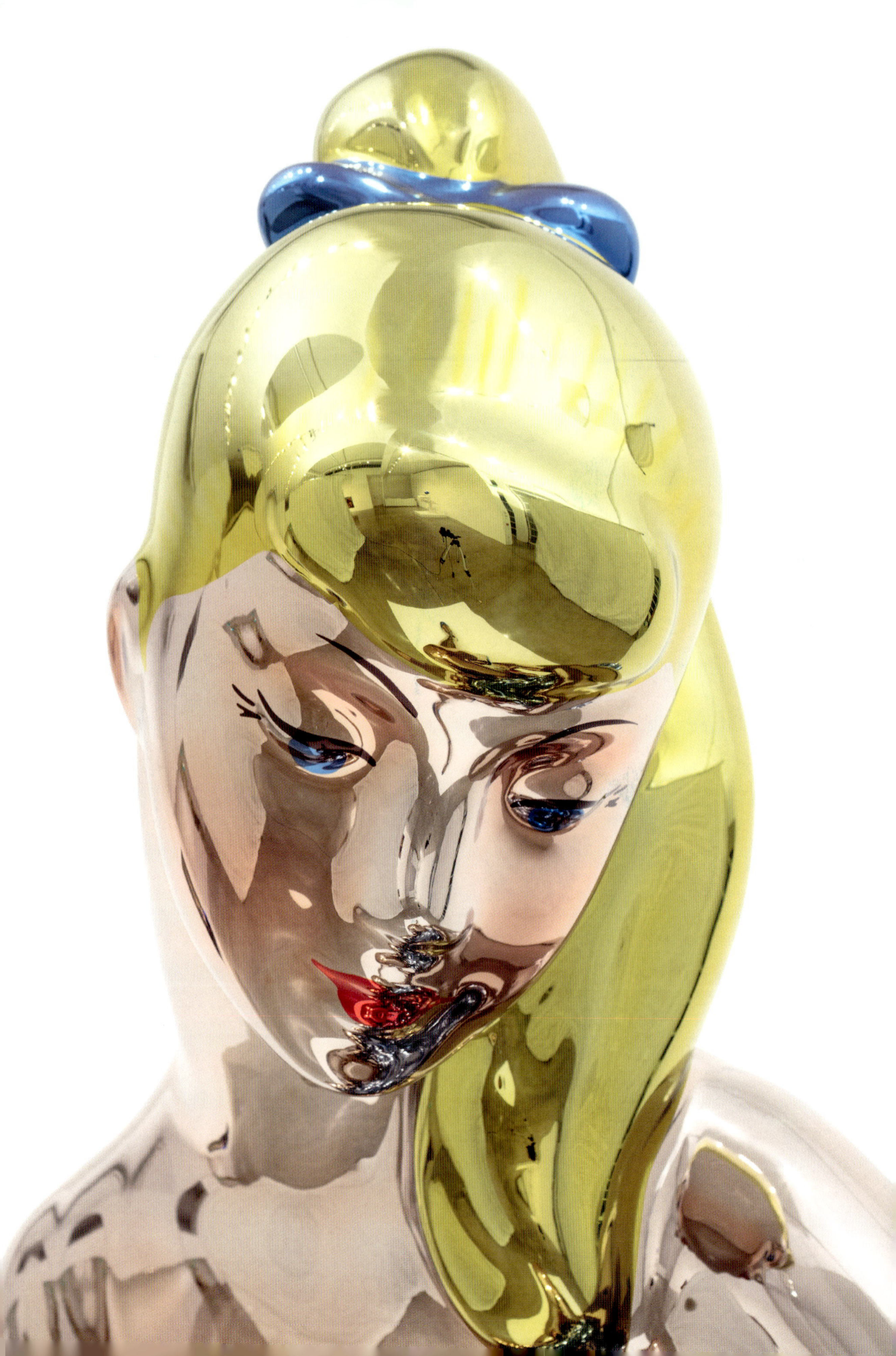

— **Xa Sturgis:** First of all thank you, Jeff, for being here and also for participating in the show at the Ashmolean. I suppose my first question is what is it that excites you, if anything, about the idea of seeing your work in the context of the Ashmolean, the world's oldest museum, with a collection that spans from antiquity to the present day?

— **Jeff Koons:** Well, the collection. But also its position as the birthplace, really, of the idea of a museum. That's really thrilling. There's also the community around the Ashmolean, its different curators and your involvement with the arts. So I couldn't think of a better place to have a dialogue about art today and what it can be.

— **XS:** There's a famous story about Picasso in the Louvre, looking around at the works of art of the past and declaring that what he does is the same thing. Is that how you see your work, as being part of this long Western tradition?

— **JK:** You know, that's a great story because I ➔

AN INTERVIEW WITH JEFF KOONS

XA STURGIS

➧ see it the same way. And what I enjoy about that story is the humanism. And it *is* the same thing in that we all are giving it up to our forebears and the people who came before us. The way we're able to experience transcendence, we're able to increase our parameters, is by giving it up to their accomplishment, enjoying something outside of ourselves. And if you look at their work, you realise that they're giving it up to other people as well. And it turns out that you're really just celebrating this inner linkage. Very similar to the genes in our DNA – this amazing double helix that links everything together. Our cultural lives do the same thing outside our bodies. So yes.

— **XS:** And thinking back to your formative experience, your artistic education, how much of that happened in museums, in front of the works of art of the past? Or was your visual language developed from looking at the world around you?

— **JK:** When I was younger, I had an aunt who lived in Philadelphia. And my aunt would take me to the Philadelphia Museum of Art on occasion. I remember in Philadelphia she also took me to see the sculpture of William Penn that's on top of City Hall. It's a very large sculpture – 37 feet tall – and I would have been about five or seven years old. And the impact, the power of this sculpture (it was made by Alexander Calder's grandfather) made a big impression: the power of it, the shock and awe of this big sculpture, 37 feet tall, on top of City Hall, probably about 500 feet up in the air. You're able to walk around the base of it and to look out over a community that has such historical importance. In America, Philadelphia is the birthplace of the Declaration of Independence and so much of our history. That was a strong connection that I felt: having a sense of awe and wonderment, and at the same time a connection to a community. Now that's not exactly art history, but that's the beginning of appreciating biological responses to things and an aspect of history.

— **XS:** It's not surprising, to me, that your memory is of a big public sculpture, a great public statement, rather than a painting in a museum. You have spoken in the past about the anxiety that some people feel in front of works of art. A worry that they don't know enough to appreciate what's going on, that there's some authority there that's inhibiting their response. Is that something you remember feeling in museums?

— **JK:** Well, I didn't go to a lot of museums when I was younger. My father was an interior decorator, and I learned aesthetics from him. My parents shared a lot of experiences with my sister and I. We took trips, we had wonderful experiences together and we got viewpoints of the world. But we wouldn't go to the top cultural museums. Although they promoted very much that I follow my interest in art. I didn't know what art was, but I had an ability to draw and to paint. And so I ended up going to art school. On my first day of art school,

[opposite left]
Sculpture of William Penn before being mounted onto the roof of Philadelphia City Hall.
Mechanical Curator collection

[opposite right]
Skyline of Philadelphia from the air with the statue of William Penn on top of Philadelphia City Hall.
Photo: phl_stoner, 2016

I didn't go to a lot of museums when I was younger. My father was an interior decorator, and I learned aesthetics from him.

[previous page]
Detail of *Seated Ballerina*, 2010–15
© Jeff Koons. Photo: Fredrik Nilsen Studio. Courtesy Gagosian

I got on a bus with the other students and we went to the Baltimore Museum of Art. They have the Cone sisters' collection, and there is a great Impressionist and Modern collection there: Matisse, Cézanne and Picasso. When I saw the exhibition, I realised that I knew practically nobody. I knew Picasso, but I didn't know Cézanne; I really wasn't familiar with Matisse; someone like Braque I absolutely wouldn't have known. But I felt like I survived that moment, and I know that it had a very big impact on me because I always want to create an art through which the viewer would realise that they were perfect. Art is about empowerment. It's about an experience where you come into contact with the essence of your own potential. That's what is important. Any other information - knowing a lineage of history or this or that artist's name - that's something different. That's telling you about the time, the setting, but what's really relevant is the essence of your own potential. That's really what art is.

— **XS:** You say you *survived* your visit to the Baltimore Museum of Art. Were you sensing that potential of art then, or were you actually feeling that this was a scary place to be, somewhere that was anxious- making?

— **JK:** I'm sure I felt a sense of inadequacy, a sense of 'wait a minute, I don't know anything here'. I remember trying out for football one time, and I didn't know anything about football. And I just went 'okay, I'd like to try out for the team'. I was cut the first day. If you don't know the rules to the game, there are so many other people who do that you're just eliminated. I didn't want that same experience to happen to me in art, and I didn't let that happen. But I see that it happens to people all the time. I could see it happening to the other students around me; they just fell by the wayside. So I wanted to keep in front of me that art is always about empowerment. It's about self-empowerment and your ability to empower other people.

— **XS:** Thinking about your *Gazing Ball* paintings that you made relatively recently, what lies behind the selection of the images that you've used for those paintings? Are they works that you know well and love, or is there some other reason?

— **JK:** I have always loved Dada and Surrealism. And if you look at my work you can see that montage has had a big influence on me; I have always montaged different images together to create sculptures and paintings. Since around 2000 I started to relate this to my interest in biology. I love John Dewey, the philosopher; he really speaks about life, what it is. It's the experience of our internal biological existence and its relationship with the external world: the impact our biology has on the external world and vice versa, the impact that the external world has on our biology. I was also thinking about human history. The truest narrative we have of human history is in our genes, in our DNA. This type of linkage that exists internally within our biology also

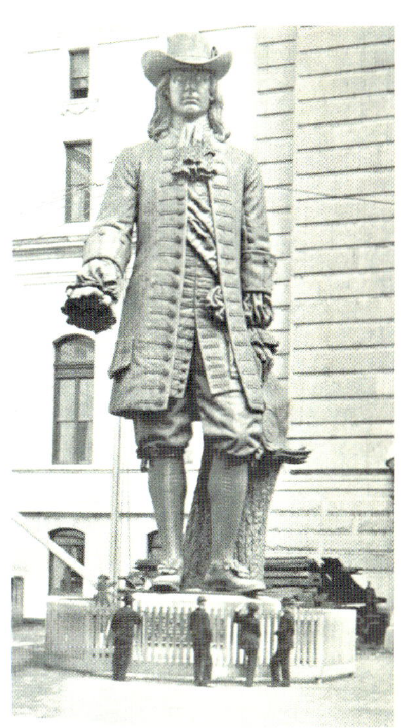

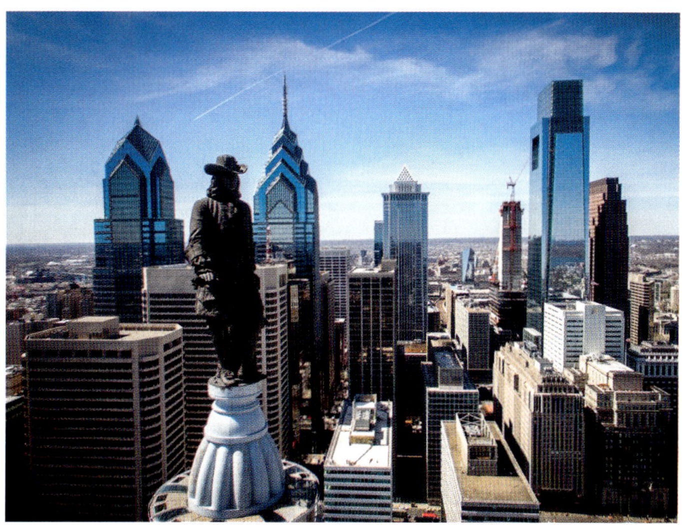

exists externally; I wanted to manifest that and bring it out into reality. I wanted to make works that are about human montage and to be able to show Titian with Ovid or Manet in connection to Watteau and Velázquez and Raphael, to go back through time.

— **XS:** So it's a form of time travel: the images that you select are about this history and about this connection.

— **JK:** My work has always celebrated the metaphysical. One of the definitions of the metaphysical that I like is by Nietzsche, who says that the metaphysical is the right here, right now: it is the eternal and the future. And so these works are the reflection in a gazing ball. That reflection is the right here, right now, and it is the affirmation of us. But then also these objects are being affirmed. And when they're affirmed, they fall in the shadows of themselves and you go right into Platonism and the realm of ideal forms and the idea, the eternal. And the future is the essence of our own potential. So a work like this is very much like one of my *Equilibrium* tanks. It's pre-birth and of this moment, but is also an essence of afterlife and death.

— **XS:** So the classical sculptures here, or the great paintings by Titian and Rubens and others, are they in a way archetypes for you of this Platonic ideal? Or are there particular reasons for particular paintings and works of art?

— **JK:** Well, the works are from the canon of Western art history. But in saying that, we realise that that canon is influenced not only philosophically from the East, but also by imagery from the East. So it really turns out to be

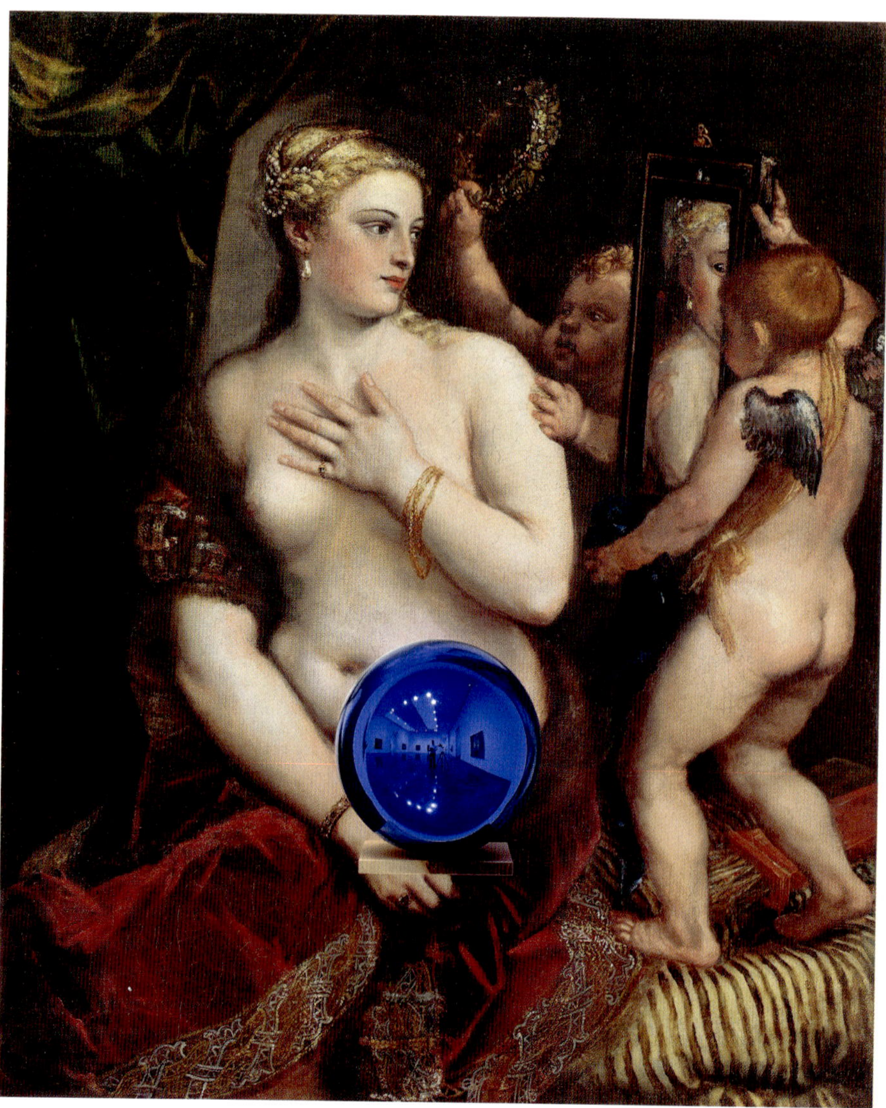

Gazing Ball (Titian Venus with a Mirror), 2015
© Jeff Koons
Photo: Tom Powel Imaging

more universal and global. But I think of these images as my own cultural DNA.

— **XS:** One of the surprises to me looking at the selection of artists is that Titian and Rubens and Van Gogh and Manet are all great gestural painters. One of the thrills for me of looking at a Titian is that sense of connection with the artist actually making it. Is that something that excites you about these paintings? Because obviously when you remake them you record that gesture, but you don't recreate that gesture.

— **JK:** I come from a tradition of ready-mades.So just as in the past where maybe I've worked with an object, I'm working with images of a Titian or a Rubens. But in the end they are unique works unto themselves. They are the *idea* of those paintings; it goes into Platonism, like an ideal form. Because even a *Gazing Ball* painting is still a gazing ball painting. It's an ideal form in itself. It's different from a painting. But it is about the aspect of transcendence, the excitement of the work. I do enjoy looking at Titian. I become excited about the way he uses light and space, the sensuality of his work. But I also love the sense of life cycle and mortality, and how, as Titian also starts to lose his vision, the paintings become broken up even more in the way the brushwork is done. And so any type of humanism, that informs us of what it means to be a human being: it shows our connective quality to our past, and our ability to be able to inform and to celebrate and to lay a framework for future generations. That's what I become excited about. Biologically, that's what makes me tingle.

— **XS:** You've used ready-mades throughout your entire career. What is it about the ready-made that, for you, makes it such a potent weapon? Although 'weapon' may not be the right word.

— **JK:** They're metaphors, and every object is a metaphor for people. It's a metaphor for self- acceptance. And then, once you're able to accept yourself, you're able to go out into the world and you're able to accept other people. And they're metaphors for us. They're a way to show attention and care, and to be able to communicate with people – to give a sense of familiarity so that they're at ease with the environment and the information at hand. I find it lets you place an individual in a more open state for communication.

— **XS:** One aspect of the ready-made is that it's a familiar thing that is then being used and transformed in some way – yet this is not entirely comfortable; it can even be uncomfortable. So I'm not sure they always put you at ease.

— **JK:** The ready-made has a great history, and [Marcel] Duchamp is amazing. The power that he instilled in the idea, the ready-made, by turning everything upside down; he had a dislocative way of putting something into the context of art. But the ready-made has always been there throughout history. People would come across things and they would use them. If a temple was

My work has always celebrated the metaphysical. One of the definitions that I like of the metaphysical is by Nietzsche, who says that the metaphysical is the right here, right now: it is the eternal and the future.

close to your home and it fell down and there was a piece of marble there, you could use it above your door and so you just fitted it there. It was ready-made, it was pre-carved and you could place it there. There's a long tradition of this accessibility of objects and things that have come before. It's happened throughout history.

— **XS:** Do your ideas follow the object, or do you have an idea and then look for the appropriate object to make into a work of art? Or does the object come first and then projects develop from that?

— **JK:** I perform very intuitively. So I follow my interests, and focus upon them. I think that's the only thing that any individual can really do in life. If you do that, your inspiration never fails – it will always take you to a place where time and space bend and you connect with the universal. Because once you really focus on your interests, you realise the abundance of the information. Everything's here: it's all around us. And you realise that the ability of almost total consciousness is so close at hand. You become very aware just how close it is.

— **XS:** And so what's going on when you remake a ready-made? Some of your things that appear to be ready-made are actually incredibly complicated and technically challenging sculptures in painted metal. For you, is that doing something very different? Or is it simply trying to be that thing in a way that is more long-lasting than an inflatable, for example, might be?

— **JK:** I love sense perception. The artwork that I've always enjoyed and respond to is work that excites my senses. It gets everything going. There's a sense of enlightenment, a strong sensation. So I'm pulled to objects that can supply a heightened sense perception, and that will come from a very intuitive process. But then, by thinking about that object that I'm drawn to, I'll start to see how it's interconnected to other images – other objects that it shares a vocabulary with or with which it can very easily be placed into a narrative that's interesting. So it really unfolds itself.

— **XS:** And so that frisson of excitement around the trompe l'oeil element of your work, which makes you want to touch them to discover whether it really is Play-Doh or an inflatable or not – is that a response that you're aiming for? Or is that a by-product, if you like, of what you have created?

— **JK:** I would it say it depends. It really varies. I give a lot of time and attention to my work, and I'm known for having a certain amount of perfectionism or using a high level of craft. But I'm not obsessive about it. I don't believe in it because I feel that obsessive perfectionism is actually like fetishism. It's like a dog just chasing its tail. It doesn't go anywhere. But I believe that you can use craft to communicate to people that you care about them and respect them and want to communicate with them; you want to show them all the attention that you would like to receive in return and to show that you really care for them. And so the details that are in an object are a

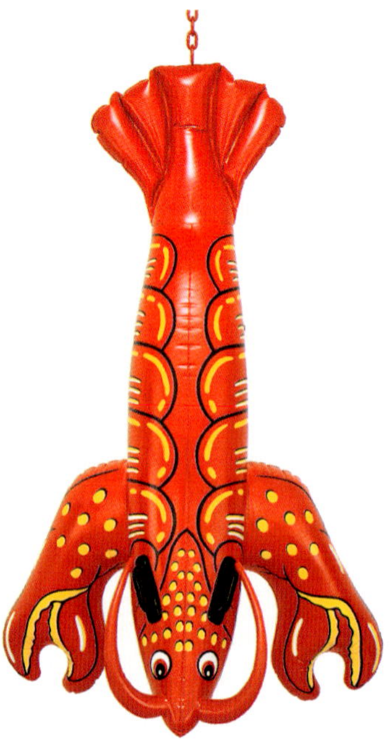

Lobster, 2007–12
© Jeff Koons. Photo: Tom Powel Imaging

[opposite]
Play-Doh, 1994–2014
© Jeff Koons. Photo: Tom Powel Imaging

metaphor for expressing that care to the individual. And both the perfection and the imperfection in the finished piece is essentially that of the viewer.

— **XS:** And so a lot of the attention to detail in some of your astonishing reproductions of historic casts or paintings would not be recognised by most viewers. But you feel that it would in some way be sensed if that attention to detail wasn't there?

— **JK:** Well, I think that if people come across an image like this [pointing to *Gazing Ball* sculpture] – I think that these are supercharged – they have something going for them. The viewer may not know what that is exactly, but maybe they just feel a little excitement or they just enjoy something about it. But I don't believe that these works are demanding anything of the viewer. It's really just about the perception that they have of themselves and of their own potential. If viewers are curious about discovering more about a certain object, they can go deeper into it. But it's really about their interests and what they're curious about at that moment.

— **XS:** So thinking about whether your works are demanding a lot of the viewer, your paintings in your

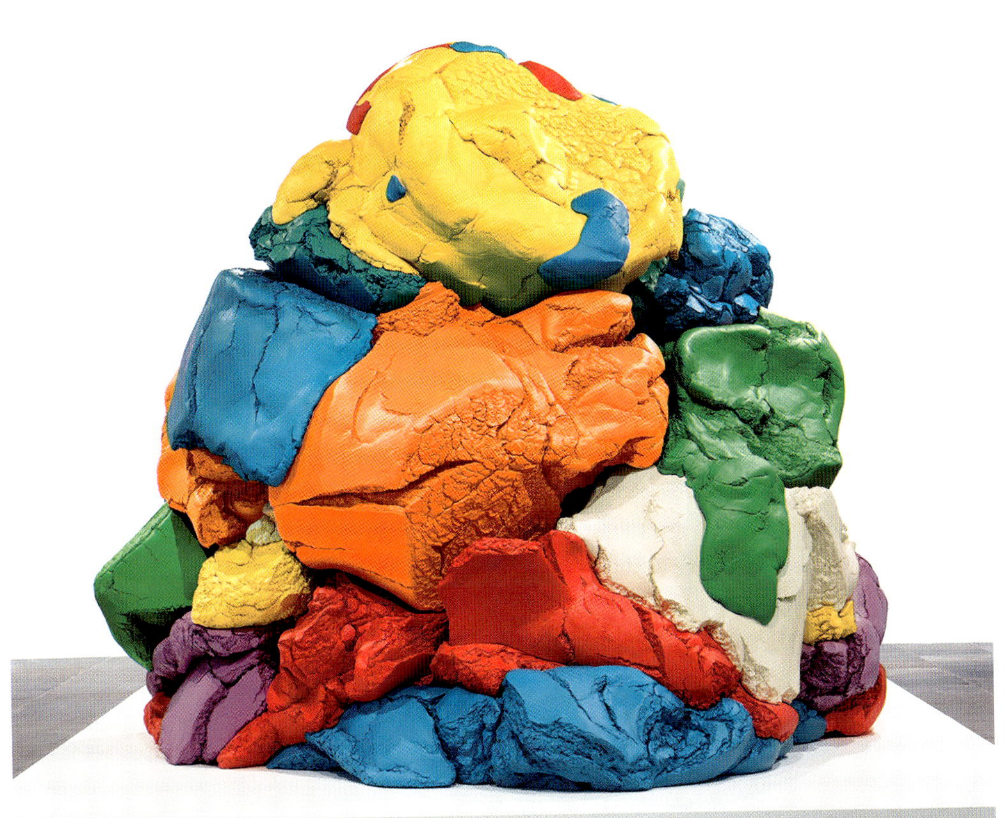

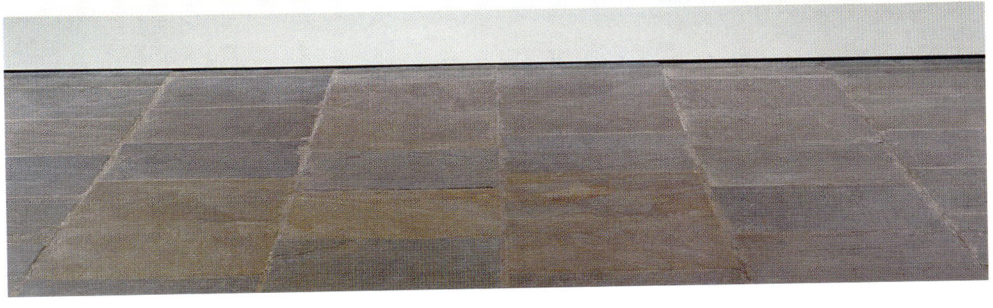

Antiquity series are so layered. They allude to different classical sculptures which may or may not be known. But if you know what they are, it adds a certain amount to how one might look at the painting and interpret it. But do you think that knowledge is not necessary for a viewer: that the painting does reveal all of itself for those who look?

— **JK:** Absolutely. It's not necessary at all. The way art empowers is to communicate to the viewer that it's all about this moment: they don't have to be prepared in any manner. Their own cultural history is perfect. Their whole history. Everything about the viewer is perfect. Everything is about this moment forward. Connoisseurship is really beautiful. It's not something which is about disempowering people; it's just pure joy for the self, for the individual. It's like enjoying a flower and then maybe becoming just a little curious about what family of flowers it's from, or whether you can transport that flower and replant it somewhere else. It's about the joy of information because of the pleasure of the connectivity.

— **XS:** So for me, looking at the trajectory of your work, it seemed like a significant shift when you moved from popular imagery, what one might call 'low art', to classical imagery and 'museum art', if you like. Did it feel like a shift to you? What triggered that move to look at the works of classical Greece, for example?

— **JK:** Really, the appreciation of humanism and to try

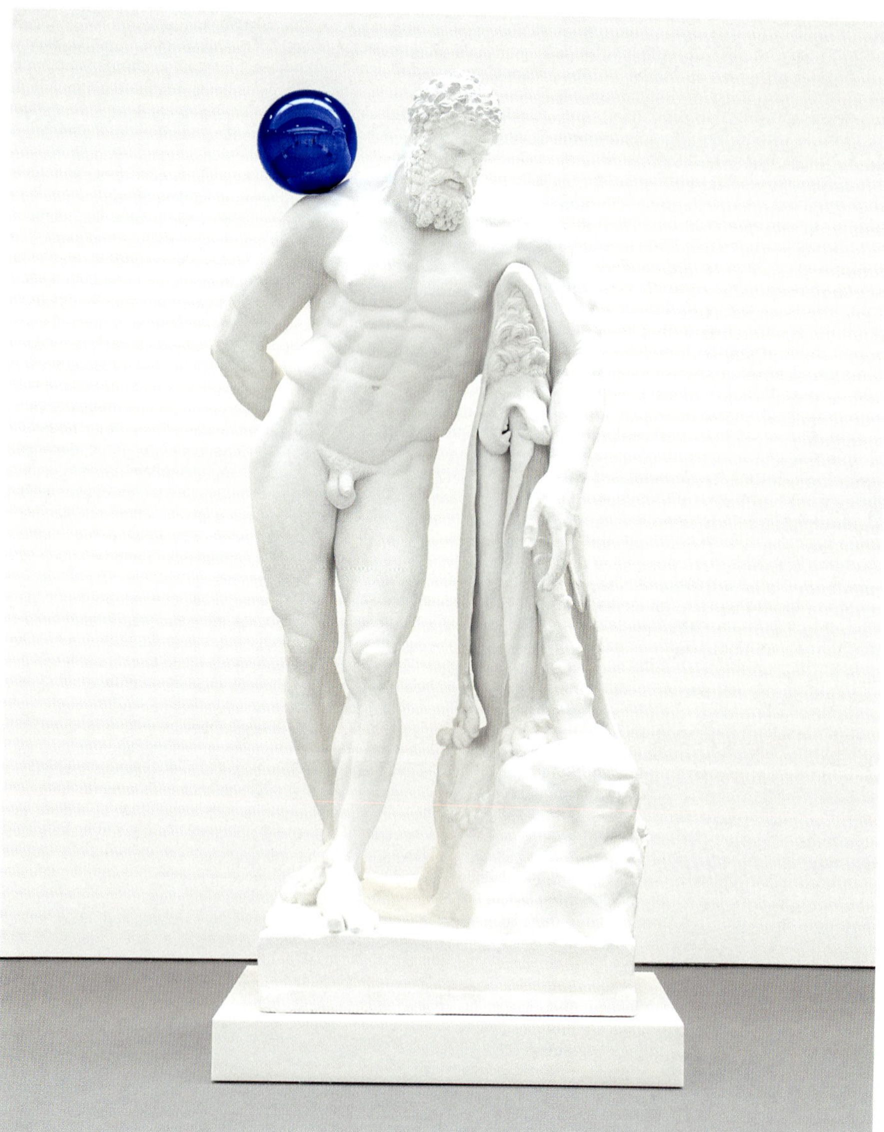

***Gazing Ball (Farnese Hercules)*, 2013**
© Jeff Koons. Photo: Tom Powel Imaging

[opposite left]
***New Shelton Wet/Drys Tripledecker*, 1981**
© Jeff Koons. Photo: Douglas M. Parker Studios, Los Angeles

[opposite right]
***New Hoover Convertible*, 1980**
© Jeff Koons. Photo: Douglas M. Parker Studios, Los Angeles

to continue a dialogue about this subconscious in our information that's deep and profound within us. Because if I'm working with a piece from the antique, for me it's embedded with a lot of information. It's about different societies, what was important to them, what information they had again that was transported biologically, what came from their cultural environment. And my work emphasises that. It emphasises the relevance of both the internal, what we carry with us in our genes, and then what comes about through interaction, our cultural interaction. It seems more enlightened than participating in a dialogue about the new or just everything about this moment. I find it much more interesting to be looking at a vaster picture. And you can get more of an idea of what our potential is as individuals by looking at a broader past, of seeing what we've held in relevance of being important to us. I love to look at the idea of sexuality not just maybe from this moment in time, but to pull back and to look at sexuality as far as you can, from the division of the first amoeba or the first division of a cell.

— **XS:** And is that what the layering in the paintings is about as well? Is that about this passage of time?

— **JK:** Yes, it would be about time. It would be about information. It would be about trying to have multiple views at one time. There's a tradition of working with different transparencies. Picabia [Francis Picabia, 1879–1953] worked with transparencies, and Picasso

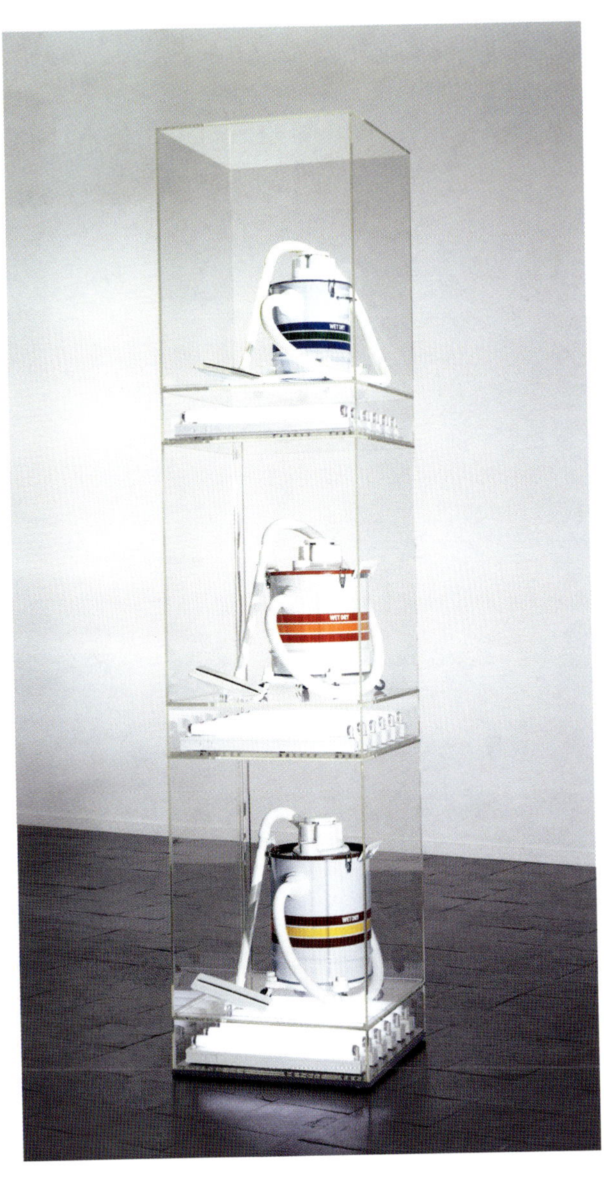

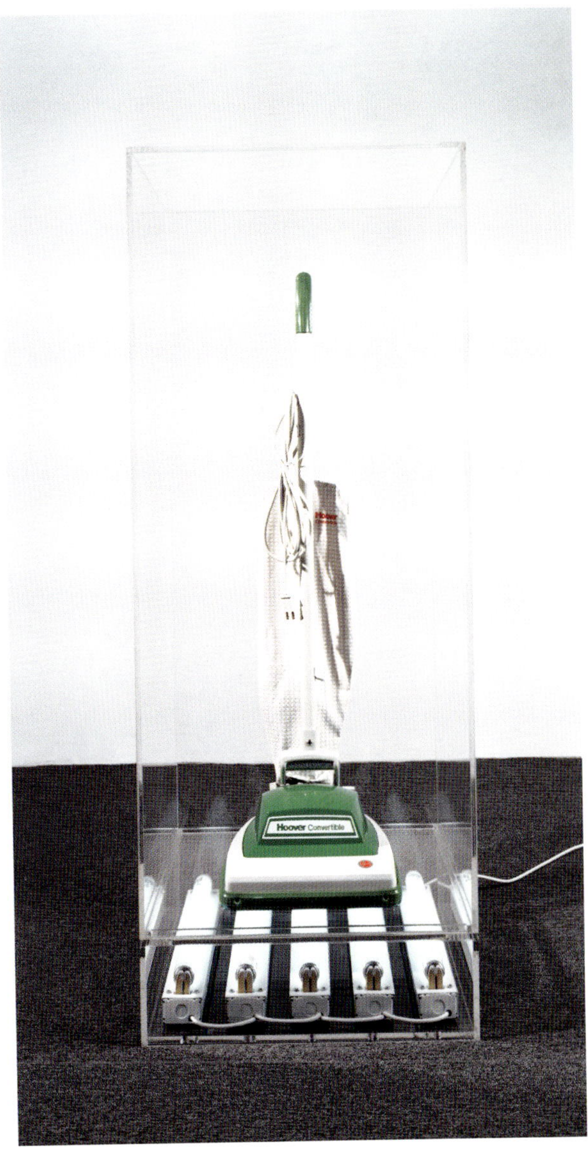

worked with Cubism, with its different type of angles. It's a way of representing multiple images at one time and of being able to bring them together while creating an image unique in itself.

— **XS:** One of the great works in the show is the wonderful *Balloon Venus*. Would you mind just telling me how that came into being?

— **JK:** My works have always enjoyed an aspect of air. I worked with vacuum cleaners, and even before the vacuum cleaners I worked with inflatables - inflatable flowers. In my *Equilibrium* tanks the basketballs are filled with air, and so are my *Balloon Dogs*. So the idea of breath has been very important to my works. I think it comes about just defining this balance of interior/exterior. You breathe in and you inflate. You pull the external realm into yourself, and you inflate.

Breath is a symbol of life energy. And when you exhale and it returns to the exterior, that's a symbol of almost your last breath and of death. So just by using breath and a membrane, you can convey a lot of information and an aspect of time. To me *Balloon Venus* carries the energy of a cult-type image: something like an archaic or tribalistic type of object that a community would maybe rally around. And if you look at the balloon-like quality that comes from blowing up a vinyl or latex balloon, I would imagine that in primitive times maybe people looked at their kill and they noticed the gases were expanding in the stomach and that they could work with this type of membrane and that they would make something like a balloon Venus or a balloon dog - an object like that - for ritualistic purposes.

— **XS:** Can you actually make that Venus out of balloons?

— **JK:** It was made out of balloons.

— **XS:** It *was* made out of balloons?

— **JK:** Yes. It comes from an actual balloon that I designed. I worked with a real balloon specialist in blowing them up to create that exact shape. And I would have manipulated the shape slightly because we would have blown up quite a few of them and selected different ones; we CT-scanned and white-light scanned them. We've taken all this information to create a computerised model. But when you blow something up to about 104

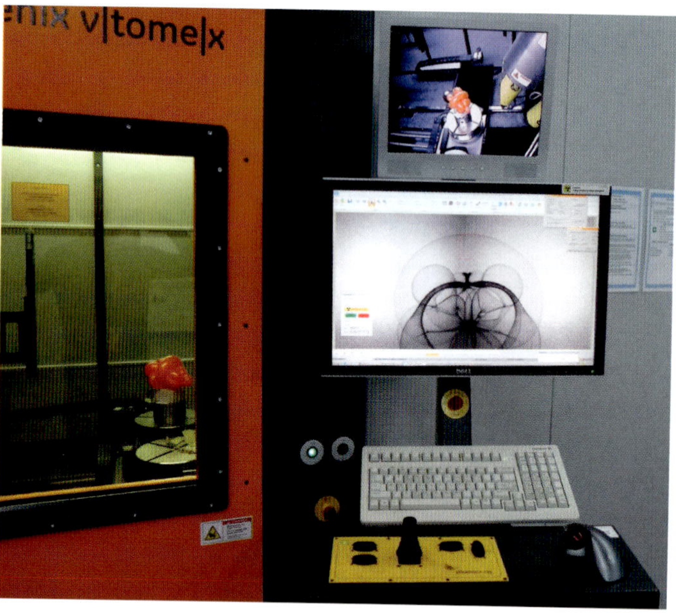

Balloon Venus, 2008–12, during CT Scan

[opposite]
Balloon Swan (Blue), 2004–11, *Balloon Monkey (Red)*, 2006–13, and *Balloon Rabbit (Yellow)*, 2005–10.
Exhibition view of *Jeff Koons – New Paintings and Sculptures*, Gagosian, New York, 9 May–29 June 2013.
© Jeff Koons. Photo: Tom Powel Imaging

inches tall, if one chamber is a little too asymmetrical, it could have an oddness that I would take the liberty of adjusting – so that nothing is completely symmetrical, but so that the asymmetry may not be off so much.

— **XS:** Let's talk briefly about the technical side of your work. I get the sense (but I may be completely wrong) that you assume everything is technically possible: that you have an idea and then it's just a question of finding out how to make it. Or is there sometimes an interesting moment where your idea comes up against what is technically possible or impossible? Do interesting things sometimes happen then?

— **JK:** I think I always come up against the fact that it's technically not possible, because I'm always pushing it and it's just something that happens. You always continue to push it and push it until you've reached a certain point – you have gone as far as technology says you can go right now. And you keep pushing to try to find a breakthrough: can a new chemical be created? Or maybe a new tool can be developed, a new way of looking at it, a new algorithm – something that can help you get past this problem that you have? But that's just a natural thing, I think, that comes along with the act of making something. It happens because you want to create something that can have an effect of channelling life's energy.

— **XS:** And so are there moments where you just abandon things because they can't be done? Or do you compromise?

— **JK:** Well, I keep pushing, and it's always a compromise. But I keep pushing for the next one. Hopefully, the next time we can get this even further. I don't stop because I'm still interested in other ideas that are taking place instead.

— **XS:** So before we end could just come back to the gazing balls and the *Gazing Ball* paintings? Because I think a gazing ball is quite a familiar object to an American audience – I think they sit in a lot of gardens in the suburbs of America – but they're unfamiliar in the UK. Can you tell me a bit about how you arrived at the idea of using the gazing ball?

— **JK:** I was brought up in Pennsylvania, where there is a large German population. When I was growing up,

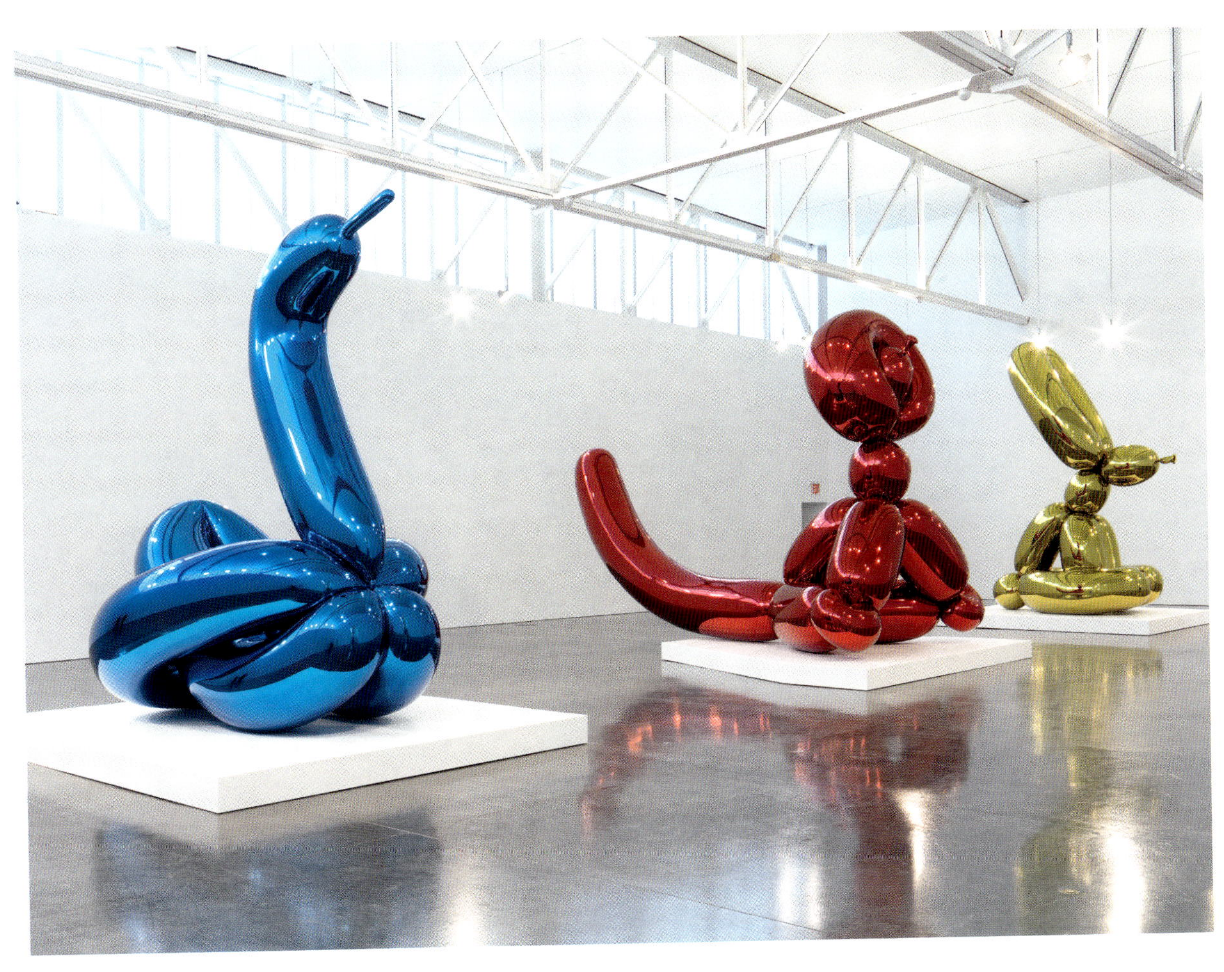

people would put gazing balls in their yards as lawn ornaments. And when you would walk by or drive by, there was a sense of a generosity, a feeling that they had done that for you. And because they're hand-blown glass balls, they reflect almost 360 degrees. So they're telling you everything they can about where you are in the universe at that the moment. And the mind is always rewarding you for that information. It always wants to know where you are in the universe. So using a gazing ball already has that going for it. I was always attracted to that aspect of generosity, the fact that the gazing ball would just be there in a yard. I always wanted to work with a gazing ball because I find it one of the most simple, pure forms that you could work with. Just this sphere. I thought about it for about 30 years before moving forward. King Ludwig of Bavaria helped to make gazing balls popular in Victorian times, although they were originally created in Venice in the 1500s. King Ludwig placed them in some of the gardens of his schlosses and helped to re-popularise them. And so today, if you go to a new garden centre or shop selling lawn ornaments, you'll see gazing balls there to purchase.

— **XS:** And so, as you've talked about them, they're obviously a device that puts the viewer into the work of art. And again you've spoken before about this idea, which is clearly true, that every work of art depends on the viewer and is completed within the viewer.

— **JK:** I think gazing balls celebrate. They celebrate the viewer's yard. They celebrate the individual viewer, but they make everything special. Now a gazing ball for sale in a garden shop could cost $19.99. I have to make approximately 350 gazing balls for each one that I'm able to bring to a quality, to be at a level, to try to communicate that the viewer can just get lost in the reflection for as long as possible. So I have to create many more to be able to get just one that has few bubbles or imperfections.

— **XS:** What happens to the other 349?

— **JK:** They become broken up and we remelt them.

— **XS:** They're not available in garden centres?

— **JK:** No. Each one is hand-blown. Again it's made from breath, so that's a bubble of human breath.

— **XS:** Thinking about viewers, it's clear that they all bring their own preconceptions, knowledge, ideas and baggage to any work of art that they come to. And for people looking at your work today, a lot of what they bring are ideas about you. Because you are, as you know, surrounded by superlatives - the most famous, the most expensive - superlatives both positive and negative. Does that noise around you worry you? Do you think its inevitable that when people are looking at a work by Jeff Koons they also have some idea of you as an individual, or maybe as a myth, in their minds?

— **JK:** I realised, early on, that it's something that just happens very naturally. I would make something, for instance I'd create my *Equilibrium* work, and I thought

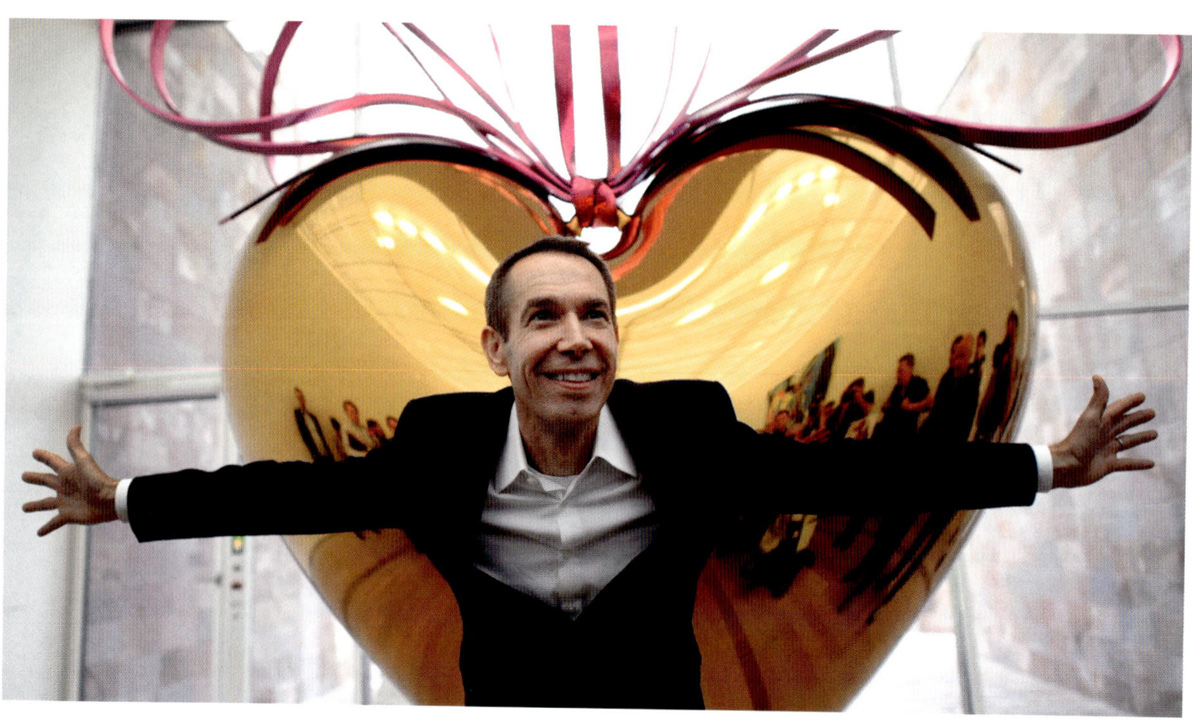

this is a body of work that is a very moral body of work, and it was about equilibrium. And it was about going for things in life: the fact that you can't ever really obtain something, but that being alive is about going for it. That's really the underlying message of the *Equilibrium* show. But I remember some reviews stating about some immoral quality to it. I was really surprised by that. I learned right away to just accept such comments, and to recognise that a lot of people don't open themselves up to art. Some people open themselves up to experience. Others don't. The only thing you can do as an artist is make the works you do, and assume the responsibility to try to communicate your intent for that work, both in the object that you make and in any type of vocabulary that you create around it. And you really can't do more than that. I know what my intentions are. I love art. Art has made my life vast. It has let me explore different interests and different experiences in life that I never would have had without art. It has let me be involved with all the human disciplines. I can be dabbling in physics, philosophy, sociology, psychology: all the human disciplines.

— **XS:** So do you have an idea of who you're making your art for? Is it for you? Is it for us? Is it for the future?

— **JK:** Well, in the beginning, I was very selfish. It was really just for me because you love this sense perception. Works of art highlighted perception. Creativity is like a drug. Duchamp would talk about it like being a drug. But art is that way. It gets these chemicals going within your body. And when you learn personal iconography, you learn how to control that and how to create these sense perceptions. And after you do that, it's more like hunting. It's like going out and getting the kill. You bring back the kill and you bring back a mammoth. And at a certain point, the focus shifts from being just the self: you also want to share that experience with others.

And so when I make something today, I make it for myself because I'm experiencing my transcendence. I'm trying to reach a higher state of consciousness. I'm trying to become a vaster human being. But at the same time, I'm trying to share that information with the viewer. You try to empower the viewer and to communicate the potential they have through art.

— **XS:** And do you worry or think about posterity?

— **JK:** I think about the life cycle. I do have children, I have a family, and so I think about longevity and all of this through that. But as far as the idea of my work itself, no. I think about it functioning today and I think about the people who are alive today and hopefully can interact with it. But then my interest just drops there.

— **XS:** Thank you very much.

[opposite]
Jeff Koons poses next to *Hanging Heart (Gold/ Magenta)* on 11 May 2012 during an exhibition preview at the Fondation Beyeler Museum in Basel.
Fabrice Coffrini/Afp/ Getty Images

Art has made my life vast. It has let me explore different interests and different experiences in life that I never would have had without art. It let me be involved with all the human disciplines.

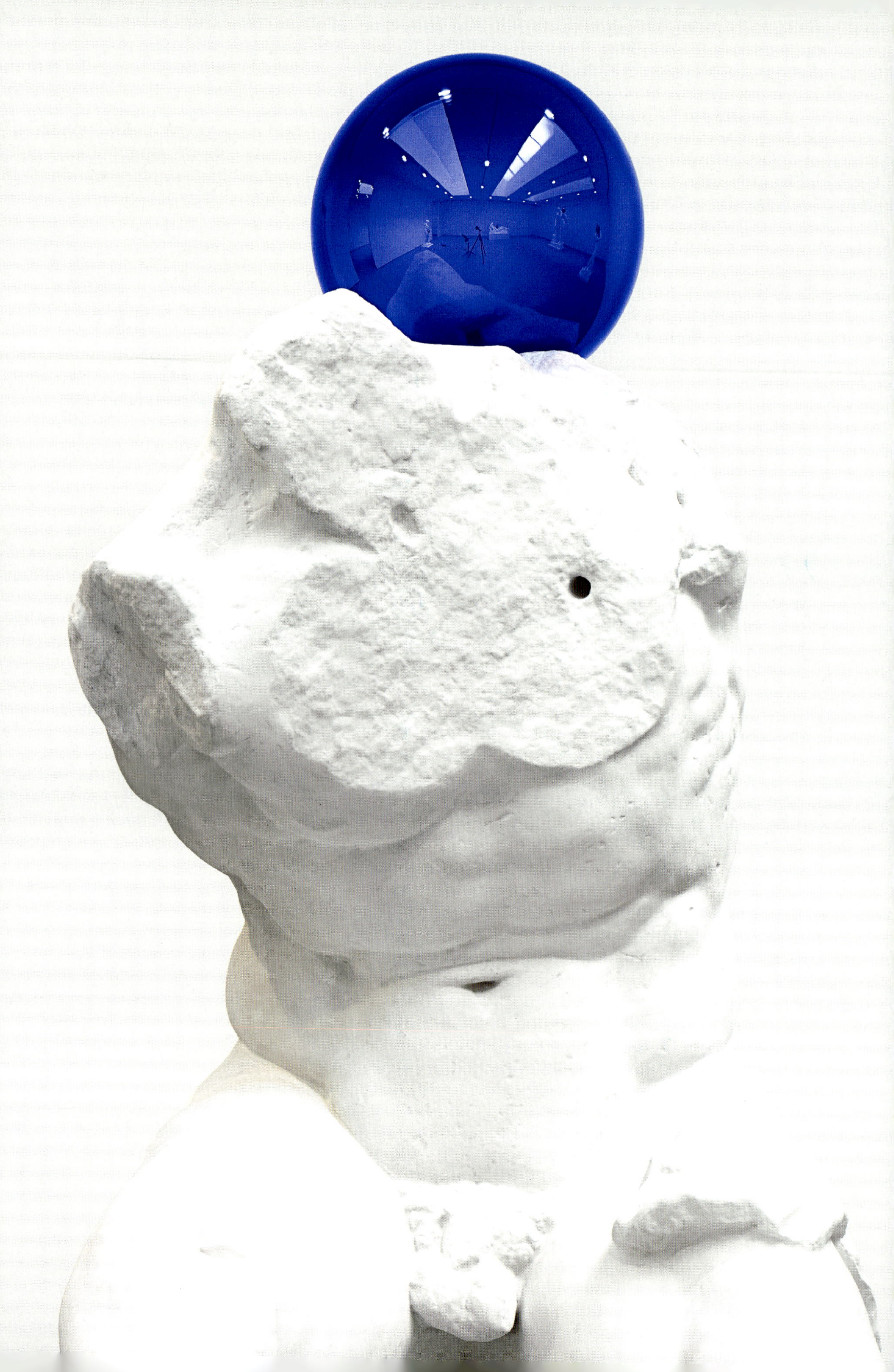

Great artists are always complex and complicated figures. Yet unlike philosophers they are also able to simplify matters, enabling understanding at a single glance by which all is revealed. *Ut pictura poesis* – 'as is painting so is poetry'– as said the Ancient Greeks and Romans. Painting and poetry indeed act as reflectors of ourselves in all their multifarious and endlessly rich manifestations.

From the very beginning mirrors have played an essential role in almost all of Jeff Koons's work. They appear in the first inflatables of 1978, in which glass flowers and other 'trite' objects picked up in cheap stores on New York's sidewalks were placed on mirrored platforms and backdrops. Subsequently many of the artist's most ambitious works, such as the *Balloon Swan*, *Balloon Monkey* and *Balloon Rabbit* shown spectacularly in New York in 2013, are finished with such shine that viewers cannot but be aware of themselves many, many times as they circle the sculptures.

JEFF KOONS AND THE SHINE AND SHEEN OF TIME

NORMAN ROSENTHAL

It was Marcel Duchamp, the principal originator of conceptualism, who famously described the viewer as essential for the completion of a work of art. In Duchamp's vision, the viewer was literally embedded within the work. However, Koons goes yet further, locating particular faculties of the viewer, as he triggers not only memories of childhood but also, more recently, more 'educated' cultural experiences as he enables us to recall classic moments of of European painting and sculpture, from the Renaissance to Picasso. He goes back even further back to pre-historic imagery, incorporating into his pictures the totemic 'sculpture' known as the Venus of Willendorf – one of the more spectacular and famous pre-historic statues found all over Eurasia and perhaps made around 30,000 years ago. Jeff Koons constantly nods and winks to the Duchamp whose name is synonymous with a form of art that makes pure and abstracted thought visible. At least that might be one way to describe the inventor of *The Large Glass* (1915–23). And that complex work leads seamlessly into the concept of the blue glass 'gazing balls' that Koons has now 'gifted' to many of the greatest masterpieces of Western European painting, from Titian and Rubens to Géricault, on to the Impressionists and beyond. Koons's subjects also encompass the classical and neoclassical sculptures, ranging from the ancients of Greece and Rome to the works of Canova, that have inspired him during visits to Western museums.

The 'gazing ball' as such is an object often to be found residing in suburban American back and front gardens and yards, perhaps poised atop a birdbath. However, the conceit of the gaze – not to mention the globe that, from its planetary centre, projects into the universe in all directions even as, mirror-like, it receives images from the space around it – has complex and ever-fascinating cultural resonance. The imagery of high and low culture is inevitably related in Koons's work, although whether he himself would accept the distinction is arguable: in his own mind both convey his central idea of the acceptance of the self as we

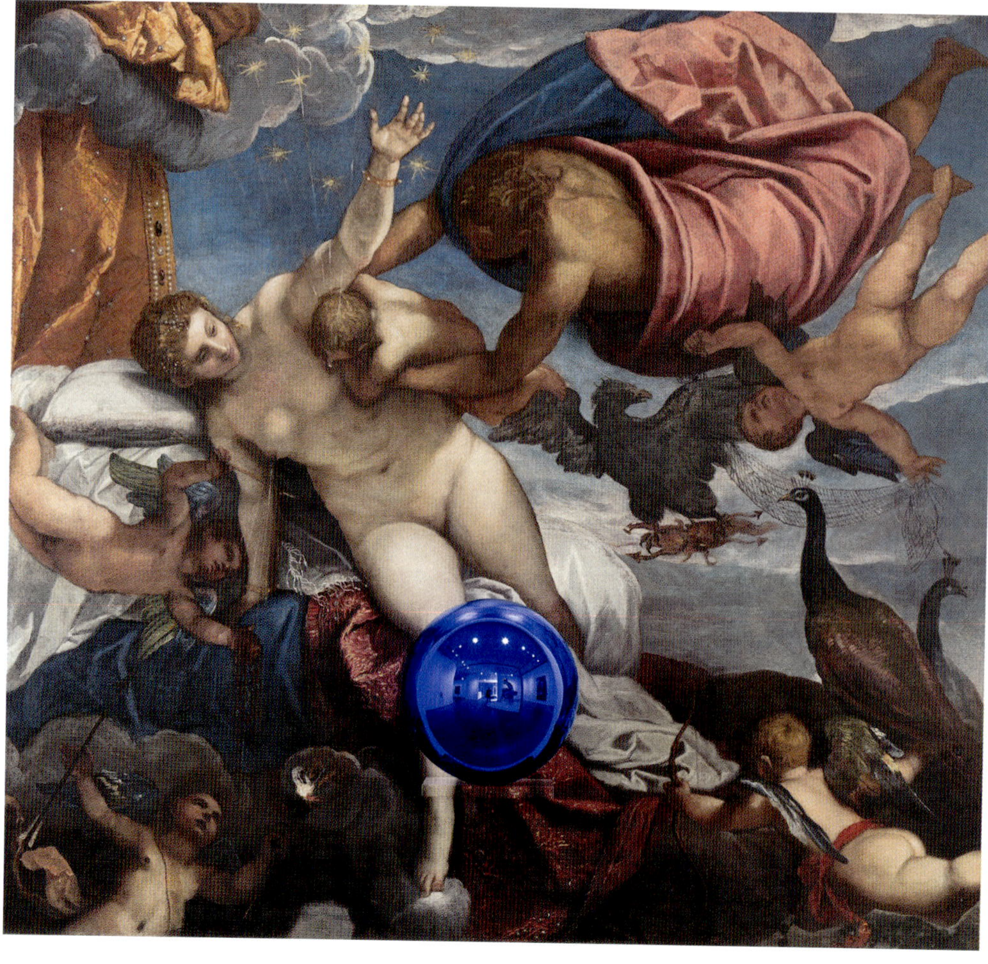

'gaze' ourselves at art. Indeed the gaze itself is part of the natural quest for the image, one that is forever and eternally changing. The viewer is constantly changing too, from day to day, minute to minute, even as the image itself – whether in this exhibition or in many of Koons's other *Gazing Ball Paintings*, as he chooses to call this body of work – undergoes its own, constantly subtle changes. This applies equally to his *Gazing Ball (Giotto The Kiss of Judas)*, 2015–16 (the original of 1304–6 is in the Scrovegni Chapel in Padua) or *Gazing Ball (Tintoretto The Origin of the Milky Way)*, 2016 (the 1575 original, now in the National Gallery, London).

Some may be tempted to call Koons's versions copies, but that is to denigrate their individual, quality-controlled execution, bewildering and almost mind-bending in its impact. In these works every nuance of colour, not to mention craquelure and other signs of ageing, has been hand-wrought by the artist and his assistants – Jeff runs his studio like that of a Renaissance master – even if not all are necessarily reproduced at a 1:1 scale. And all this in an age of photographic and laser reproduction techniques, in which the 'reproduction' of artworks can become ever more deceiving to the human eye. Where Walter Benjamin famously argued that the 'sphere of authenticity is outside the technical', here, with these evocations of great old master paintings, it is in the amazingly insane, hand-wrought technique of Koons's own studio practice that the transformation of past greatness into the present takes place. His work is akin to that of a great writer or composer, holding up a metaphorical gazing ball to transform or mirror the poetry of the ancients and investing it with new life. Consider Shakespeare as he reinterprets for his own Elizabethan age the dramas of the Ancient Greeks and Romans.

The exhibition at the Ashmolean Museum, the oldest publicly accessible museum in the world, enables us to follow the trajectory of Koons's career. It leads us from his earliest works plugged into American popular culture, the *Inflatable Flower and Bunny* bought in

[opposite]
***Gazing Ball (Tintoretto The Origin of the Milky Way)*, 2016**
© Jeff Koons. Photo: Melissa Castro Duarte. Courtesy Almine Rech Gallery

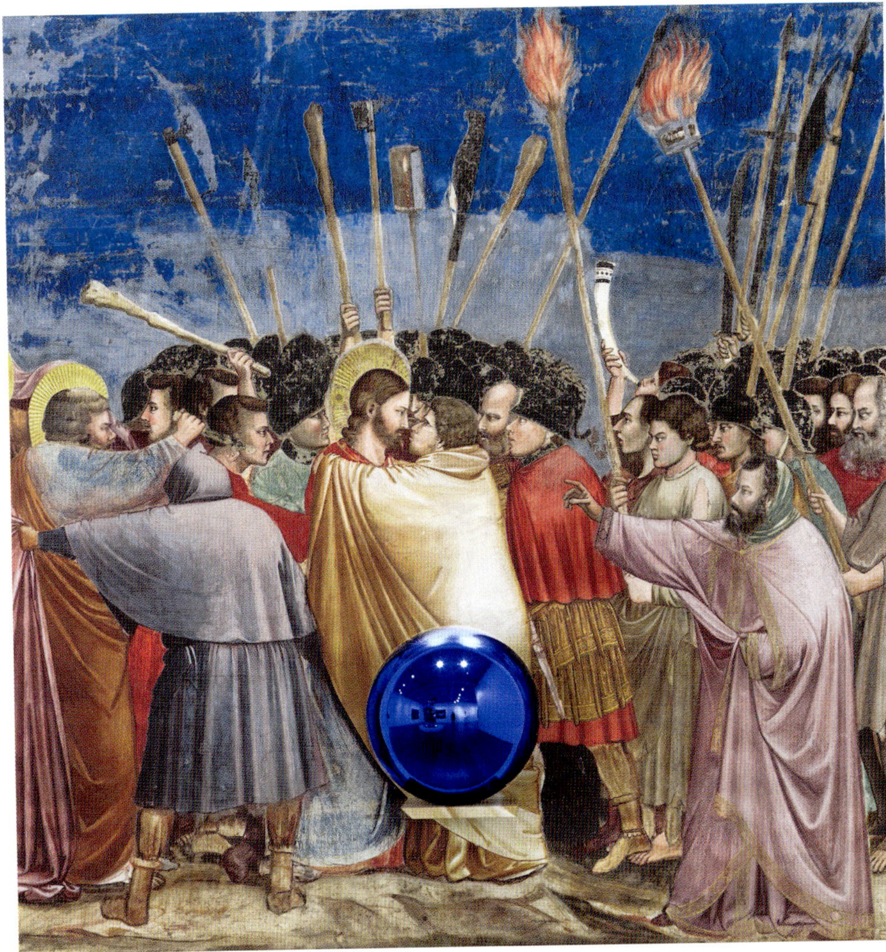

[right]
***Gazing Ball (Giotto The Kiss of Judas)*, 2015–16**
© Jeff Koons. Photo: Melissa Castro Duarte. Courtesy Almine Rech Gallery

[previous page]
***Gazing Ball (Belvedere Torso)*, 2013**
© Jeff Koons. Photo: Tom Powel Imaging. Courtesy Gagosian

the side street shops of New York in the late 1970s and positioned on mirror 'stages', the *Equilibrium Tanks* of 1985 – American Spalding baseballs 'magically' suspended (in fact placed in scientifically calibrated distilled water to allow them to float), to images of the Hulk Elvis or Bettie Page – the 'first' great American pin-up girl of the 1950s. Here we can see, more now than ever, all these figures as transformations of European and other cultures. Jupiter and Hercules, Venus and Daphne are retransmitted to us from the distant past, even as Nicolas Poussin – a highly contemporary artist to his peers and now regarded as one of the greatest old master painters – transformed the classical and biblical past for his cardinal and aristocratic clients. So did his artist peers. Who is François Boucher's *Nude on the Sofa* (1752, now residing in the Alte Pinakothek in Munich) other than the Bettie Page or Lady Gaga of her age? Both transform themselves through Koons's art into immortal heroines of beauty, as was the famous Cicciolina in her time. The goddess Aphrodite, after all, was continually reinvented by Greek artists in the third century BC and even before, each permutation drawing on subjective compositional fantasies.

We audience-participators are drawn through our own gaze into these dreams, which in turn become the art that constitutes our own visible reality. On

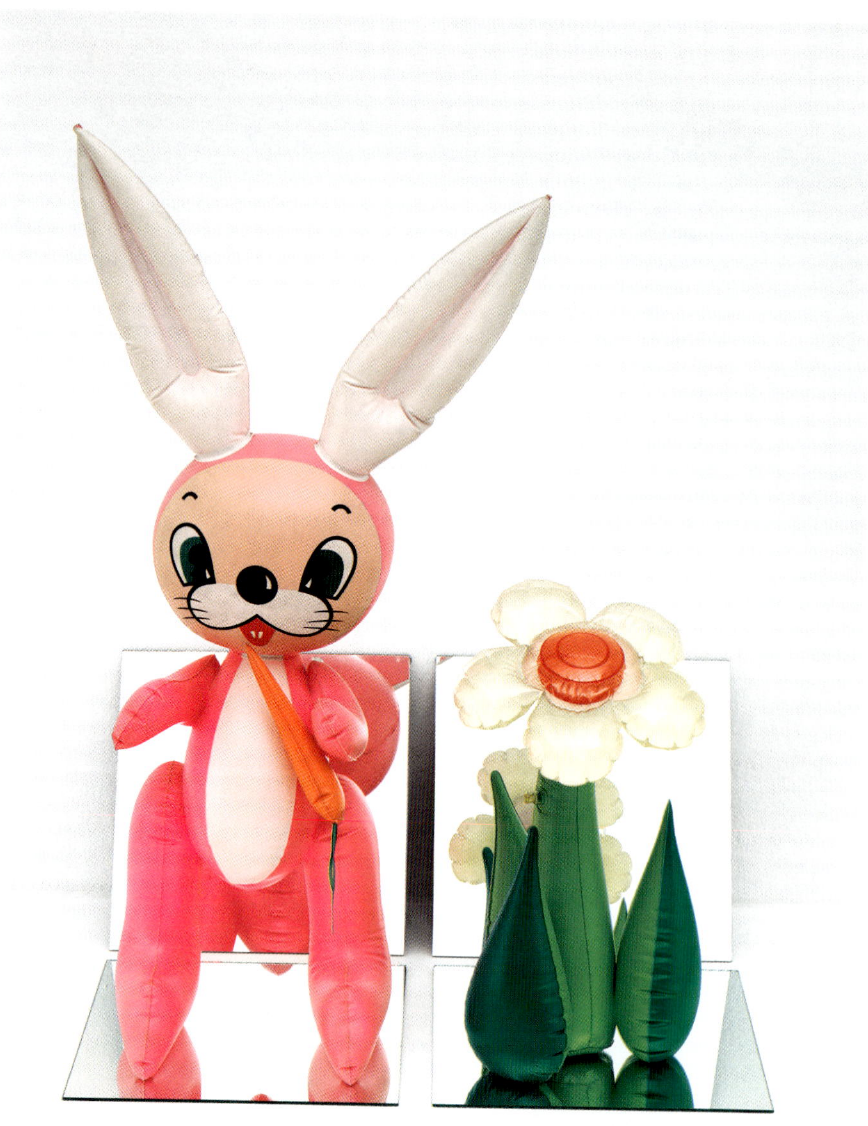

***Inflatable Flower and Bunny (Tall White, Pink Bunny),* 1979**
© Jeff Koons. Photo: Douglas M. Parker Studio, Los Angeles

the one hand the gazing ball is an alienating device. On the other it draws us to ever closer identification, even as we are overwhelmed by Koons's processes of imitation that otherwise might lead us to an unwanted confusion of authenticity and deception. The gazing ball and its placement act like any mirror, both drawing us into and pushing us away from the object, enforcing visual dialogue. The ball acts like gazing eyes, yet also resembles a universal, all-encompassing globe reaching out to the heavens. There are visual echoes in Jan van Eyck's mirror in the Arnolfini double portrait (1434) or the globe in Vermeer's painting of *The Astronomer* (1668) – or, perhaps most famously, of the mysterious ball that we find towards the bottom of Dürer's *Melancholia I* (1514) master print. But we could also invoke Bosch, Chardin and a host of other great artists. What is Picasso's classic Cubism of 1910–11, if not a vision of the world as seen through a fractured crystal ball? Do we find ourselves with all these artists in the world of perceptual science, philosophy or mystical astrology? Probably in all of these, as the artist plays serious games with perceptual and historical realities as they relate to this time – and to all time for that matter.

It was Einstein who postulated the bending of time in order to achieve true understanding of the universe. But who achieves the greater simplicity of understanding: artist or scientist? As T. S. Eliot put it so succinctly in the *Four Quartets* (1943), 'all time is eternally present'. Thus there is no distinction to be made in the quality of human culture between past and present, as Titian's *Fête Champêtre* (1509) in all its ambiguous modernity – now with its gazing ball attached in a version by Koons – makes clear in the simplest of ways. This is not without precedence in modernity. We can go even further in our sense of affinity by allowing ourselves to allude to Baudelaire as he addressed the Salon of 1846 with a preface entitled 'To the Bourgeois' – by which he meant all potential art lovers of his own time. He was himself part of the democratisation of art that took place in the nineteenth century, which today is a continuing process.

You must also be capable of feeling beauty, for just as not one of you today has the right to forgo power, equally not one of you has the right to forgo poetry. You can live three days without bread; without poetry, never; and those of you that maintain the contrary are mistaken; they do not know themselves.[1]

Of course by poetry Baudelaire is referring to the visual arts as well; in his evoking of the five senses he declares art itself to be an 'infinitely precious possession, a refreshing and warming drink that restores the stomach and the mind to the natural balance of the ideal'.[2] As Koons himself has often stated, in regard to both himself and his audience, art is about 'knowing yourself'. For him:

... the imperative of self-acceptance is so important. The motivation of art is the removal of any kind of guilt or

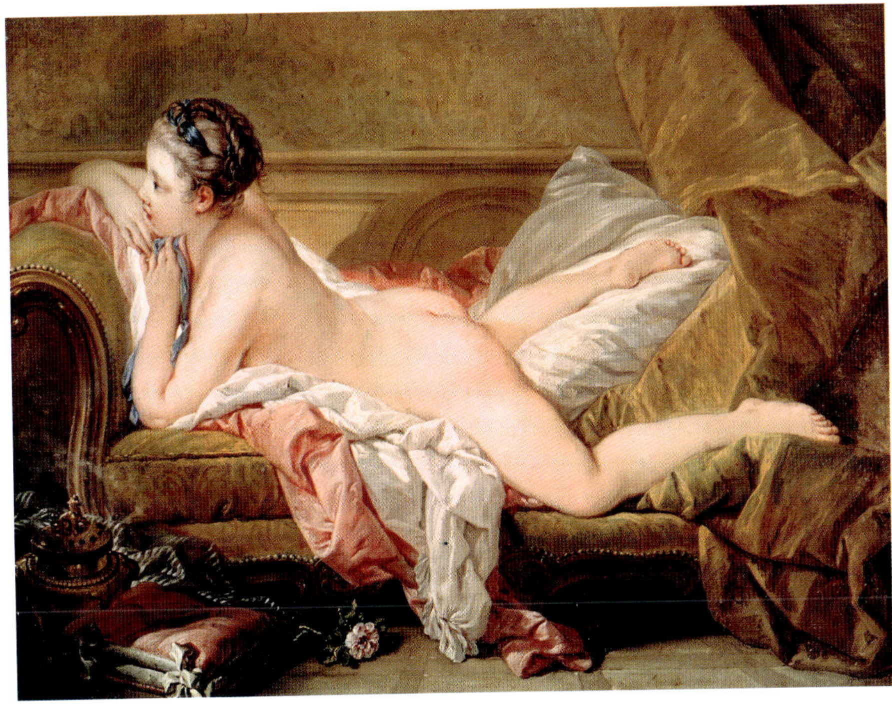

Francois Boucher (1703–70), *Resting Girl*, 1752
Oil on canvas, 59 x 73 cm
Alte Pinakothek, Munich.
Interfoto / Alamy Stock Photo

shame, or anything that people have within their history that alienates them from just dealing with the reality of themselves. It's very important to try to remove those feelings if you want to function outside the self. If you go inward you can eventually reach the bottom of the self, and art is a great tool to enable that.[3]

Baudelaire was driven by his own political context and his own contemporary ideas on the democratisation of art, which he perceived as able to reach an ever greater number of people as museums opened their doors and princely collections became more accessible. Koons, by contrast, is more interested in the biological, individualistic imperatives that enable him, as he might put it, to participate in the serious games of creativity. To do this he reaches backwards and forwards in time in order to be part of a cogent cultural present. Yet Baudelaire, though an extraordinary poet, was not a painter or sculptor. He conceived his key interest and ambition as Koons does today – namely not in the masses, but in making 'that great piece',[4] and the viewer's transformative and cathartic relationship with it.

Moving beyond the recreation of past masterpieces for our own time, Koons's work challenges artists of the past – conspicuously in the Ashmolean's exhibition Degas and Duchamp. Degas's wax model of the *Little Dancer* (1880–1) was the only sculpture he exhibited in his lifetime; after his death the world discovered innumerable waxes of dancers and women attending to their toilet in various poses, many of which ended up being cast in bronze. These are subjects that Koons has also focused on through the years in his own spectacular way, for example *Woman in Tub* (1988), part of the series known as *Banality*. Baudelaire, who throughout his life spent time with painters and sculptors as friends and equals, and as the archetypal *flâneur* of his time visited many art exhibitions, wrote a beautiful poem that reflects the relationship between art and the mirror in a powerful, classically ambiguous way:

La Beauté
Je suis belle, ô mortels! comme un rêve de pierre,
Et mon sein, où chacun s'est meurtri tour à tour,

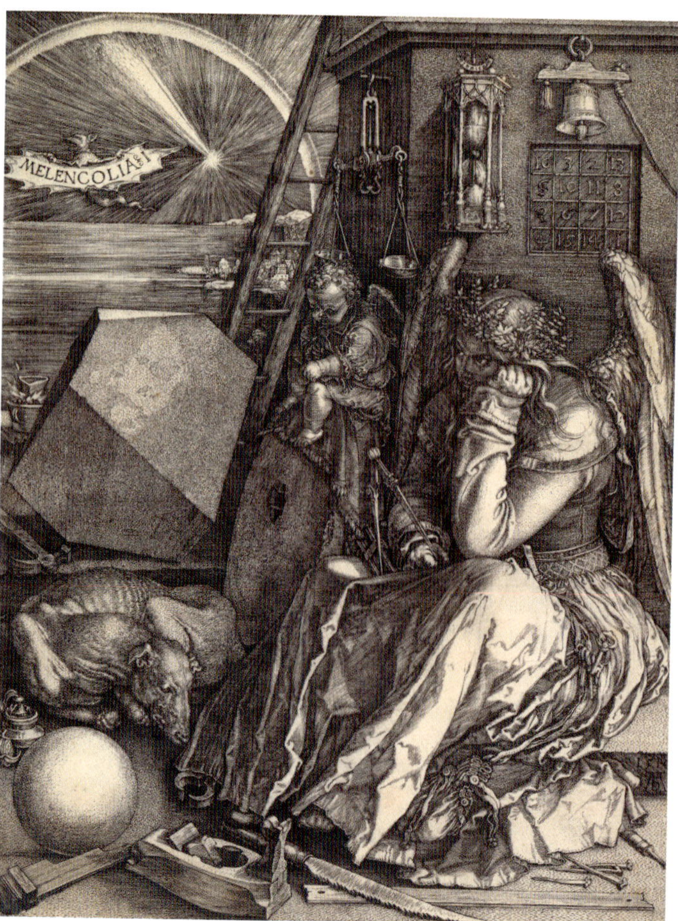

Albrecht Dürer (1471–1528)
***Melencolia I*, 1514**
Engraving, 24 × 18.5 cm
The Metropolitan Museum of Art, New York
Harris Brisbane Dick Fund, 1943

[opposite]
***Woman in Tub*, 1988**
© Jeff Koons

Est fait pour inspirer au poète un amour
Eternel et muet ainsi que la matière.
Je trône dans l'azur comme un sphinx incompris;
J'unis un coeur de neige à la blancheur des cygnes;
Je hais le mouvement qui déplace les lignes,
Et jamais je ne pleure et jamais je ne ris.
Les poètes, devant mes grandes attitudes,
Que j'ai l'air d'emprunter aux plus fiers monuments,
Consumeront leurs jours en d'austères études;
Car j'ai, pour fasciner ces dociles amants,
De purs miroirs qui font toutes choses plus belles:
Mes yeux, mes larges yeux aux clartés éternelles!

Beauty
I am fair, O mortals! like a dream carved in stone,
And my breast where each one in turn has bruised himself
Is made to inspire in the poet a love
As eternal and silent as matter.
On a throne in the sky, a mysterious sphinx,
I join a heart of snow to the whiteness of swans;

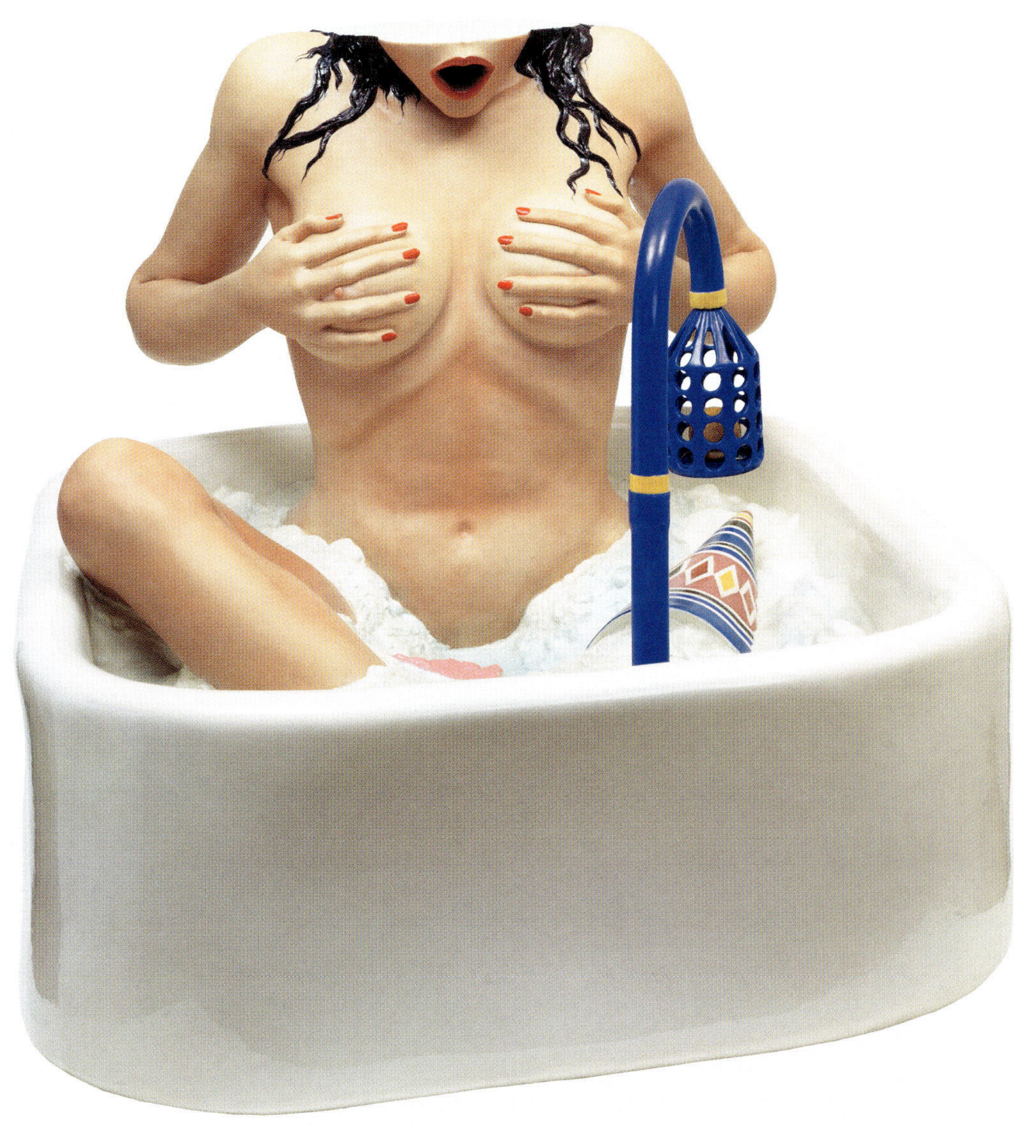

I hate movement for it displaces lines,
And never do I weep and never do I laugh.
Poets, before my grandiose poses,
Which I seem to assume from the proudest statues,
Will consume their lives in austere study;
For I have, to enchant those submissive lovers,
Pure mirrors that make all things more beautiful:
My eyes, my large, wide eyes of eternal brightness!

So perhaps we can find a beautiful equivalence between Baudelaire's pure mirrors and Koons's gazing balls? Through them Koons plays yet more similar transformative games with Duchamp's classic ready-mades – the *Bottle Rack* (1914), sometimes known as 'the bottle drier' or 'hedgehog', or the bicycle wheel. In Koons's piece we expect to see the wheel but it is no longer there: it has been replaced by a gazing ball. As Richard Hamilton comments, writing about the long-since lost original, made out of the meeting of the plainest of consumerist objects in 1913, this work was

... 'made' without the intervention of the hand of the artist (a procedure that must be clearly distinguished from objet trouvé*). The bicycle wheel was obtained and set upon a stool at a time when not even Duchamp would have dared to state it was art. It was two years later, in New York, that he identified the act as such.*[5]

Here, in Koons's work, a stool is just a stool; the gazing ball is just a gazing ball. It is what it says on the packet. If it breaks or cracks it can be replaced by another, just as Duchamp was perfectly happy to authorise replicas in his own lifetime. In this showing of his work Koons sets up a contrast between the perfectly wrought facsimile of the old master painting, the delightfully attractive high polish of the mirrored ballerina and that twentieth-century hero of the art world in whose name so much of the art of our time has evolved. For those of us willing to share in Koons's visions, he makes magical transformations of all these discoveries. The inventions of the great masters of both distant and recent art – the 'artist' of the *Venus of Willendorf*, Tintoretto and Titian, Degas and Duchamp – are born again like the ancient gods to walk once more and to sing to us anew.

Norman Rosenthal
July 2018

1 Charles Baudelaire, *Selected Writings on Art and Literature*, Penguin Books, London, 2006, p.47.
2 Ibid.
3 *Jeff Koons: Conversations with Norman Rosenthal*, Thames & Hudson, London, 2014, p.10.
4 *Jeff Koons: Conversations with Norman Rosenthal*, 2014, p.254.
5 *The Almost Complete Works of Marcel Duchamp*, Tate Gallery, 18–31 July 1966, p.43.

[opposite]
***Gazing Ball (Stool)*, 2013–16**

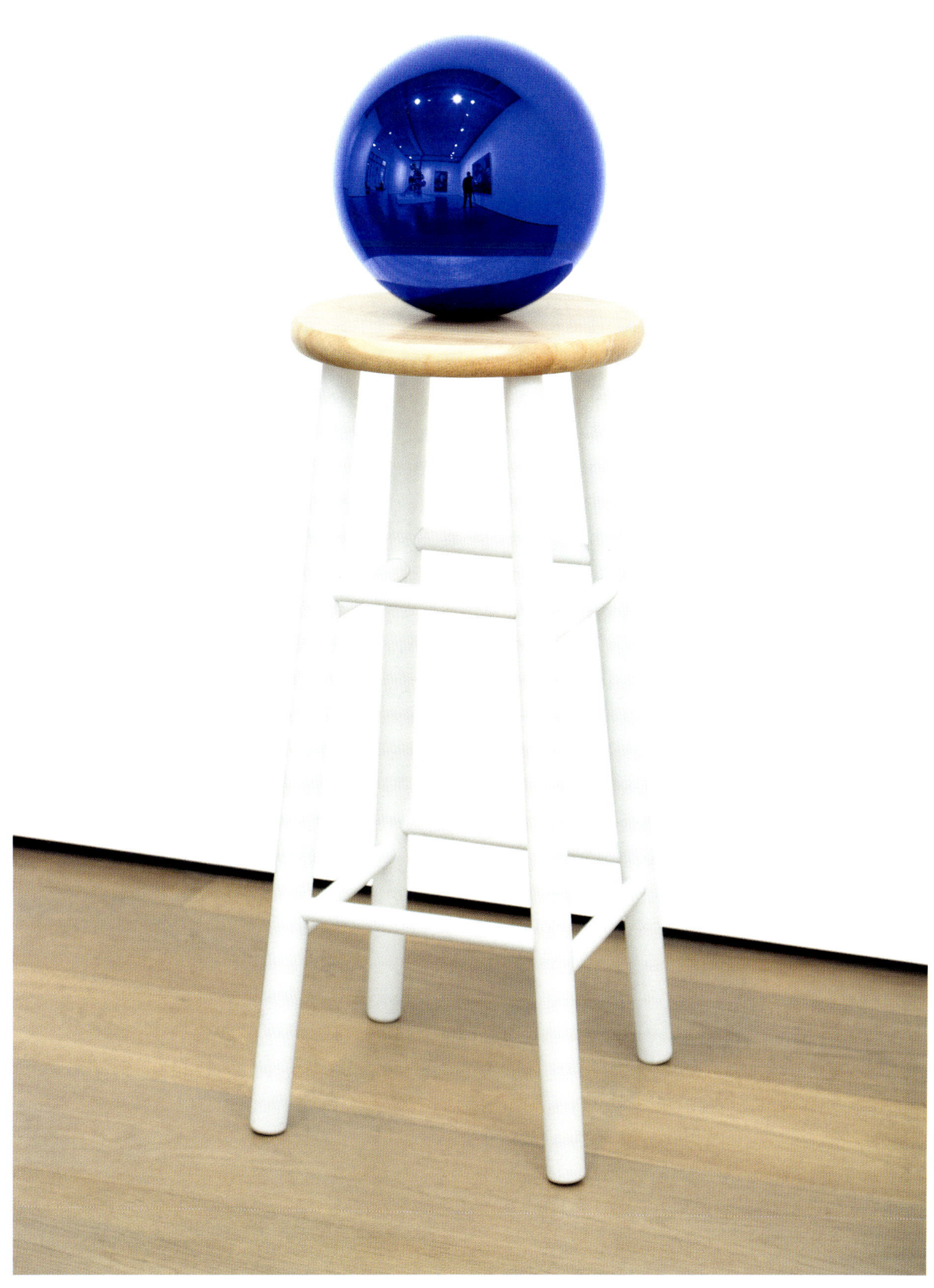

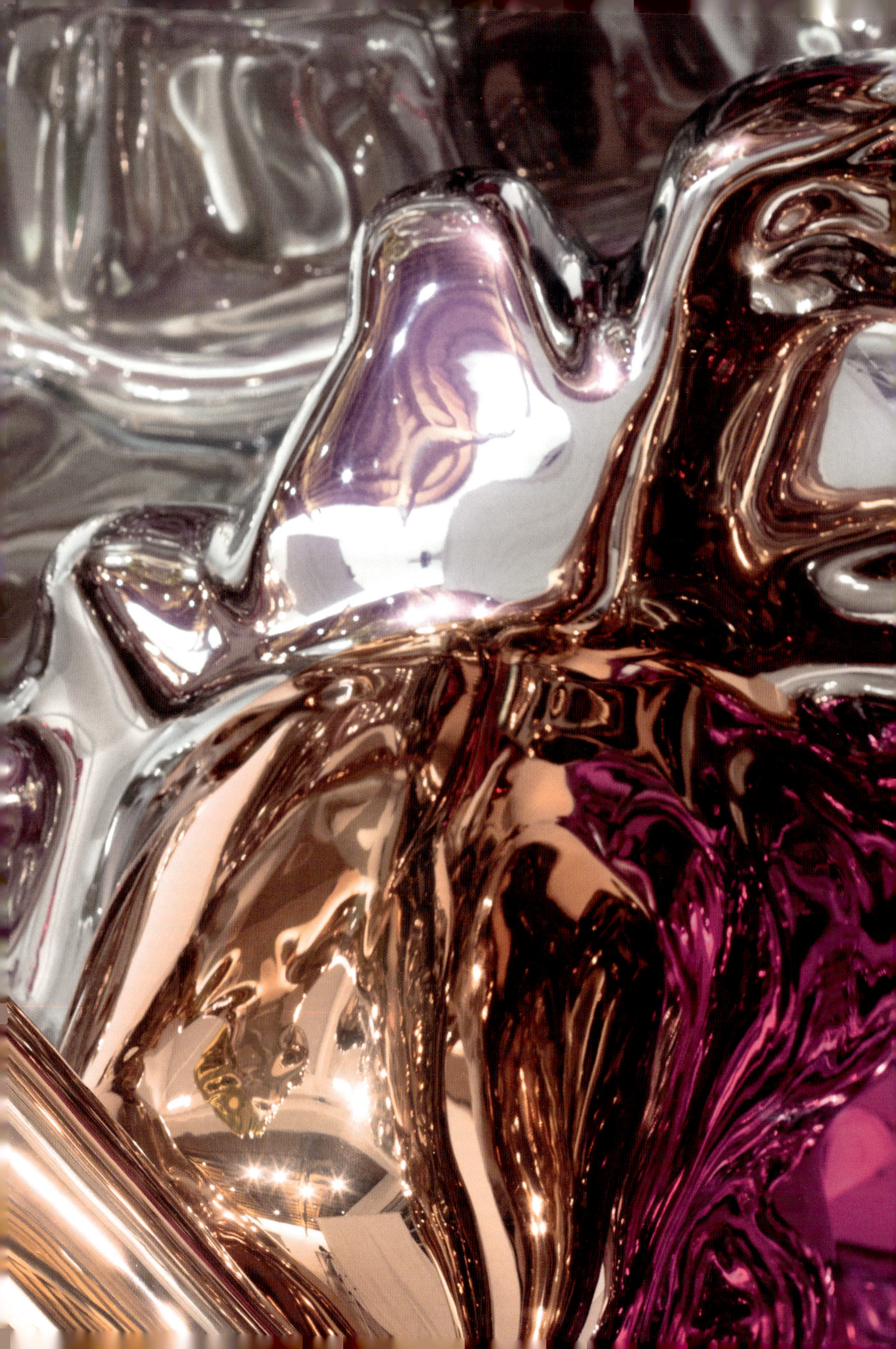

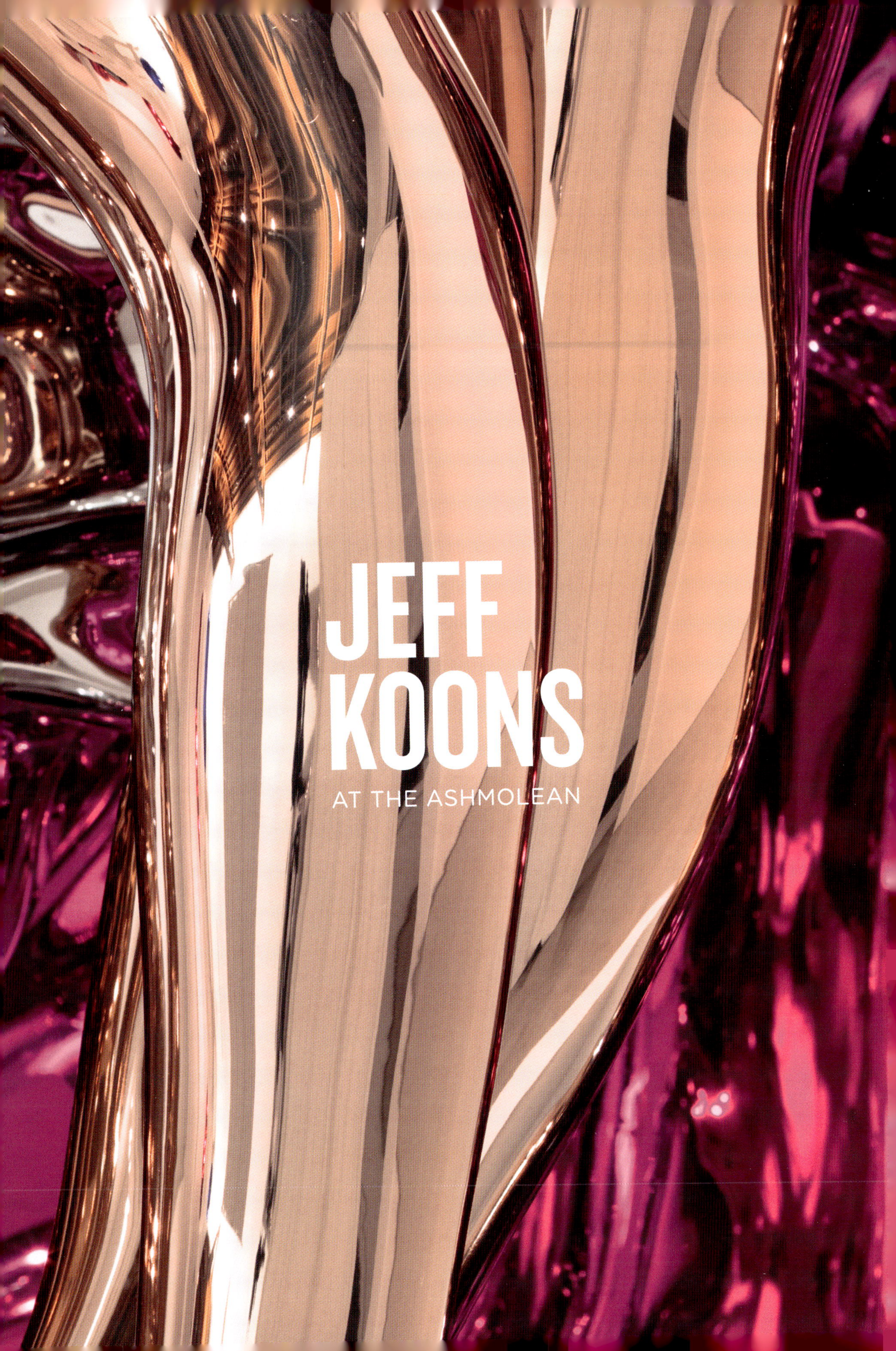
JEFF
KOONS
AT THE ASHMOLEAN

One Ball Total Equilibrium Tank (Spalding Dr. J 241 Series)
Cat. 1

Water is always very spiritual. The Equilibrium *tanks used water, and I loved that. In its very pure state it is like birth.*

Much of Koons's work is about air and breath and their intimate connection with life and death: inflatable toys, blown glass balls and, back in the 1980s, basketballs. While the famous balloon rabbit is actually made of steel, the basketball really is just a basketball – already perfect in itself and enhanced by its state of equilibrium in the water. A basketball in the 1980s was quintessentially *American*, something every teenager owned and an object that made superstars of the game's professional players.

Technically the piece was deceptively hard to make without compromising the aesthetic by adding oil to the water. The ball either floated or sank. With the help of the Nobel Prize-winning quantum physicist Richard P. Feynman, Koons devised a method that involved filling the ball with distilled water and supporting it with distilled water and pure salt. Even this does not provide permanent equilibrium, however, and the work needs to be reset as the water and salt solution mix.

As with many works from the *Equilibrium* series, Koons spent far more on producing the work than he could hope to sell it for – yet he was, and has remained, uncompromising in his attention to detail. Before his art commanded the prices it does today, he took on day jobs, even working as a Wall Street commodities broker to finance his projects.

— 1985
— Glass, steel, sodium chloride reagent, distilled water, basketball
— 164.5 x 78.1 x 33.7 cm
— Edition 2 of an edition of 2
— Collection of BZ + Michael Schwartz, New York

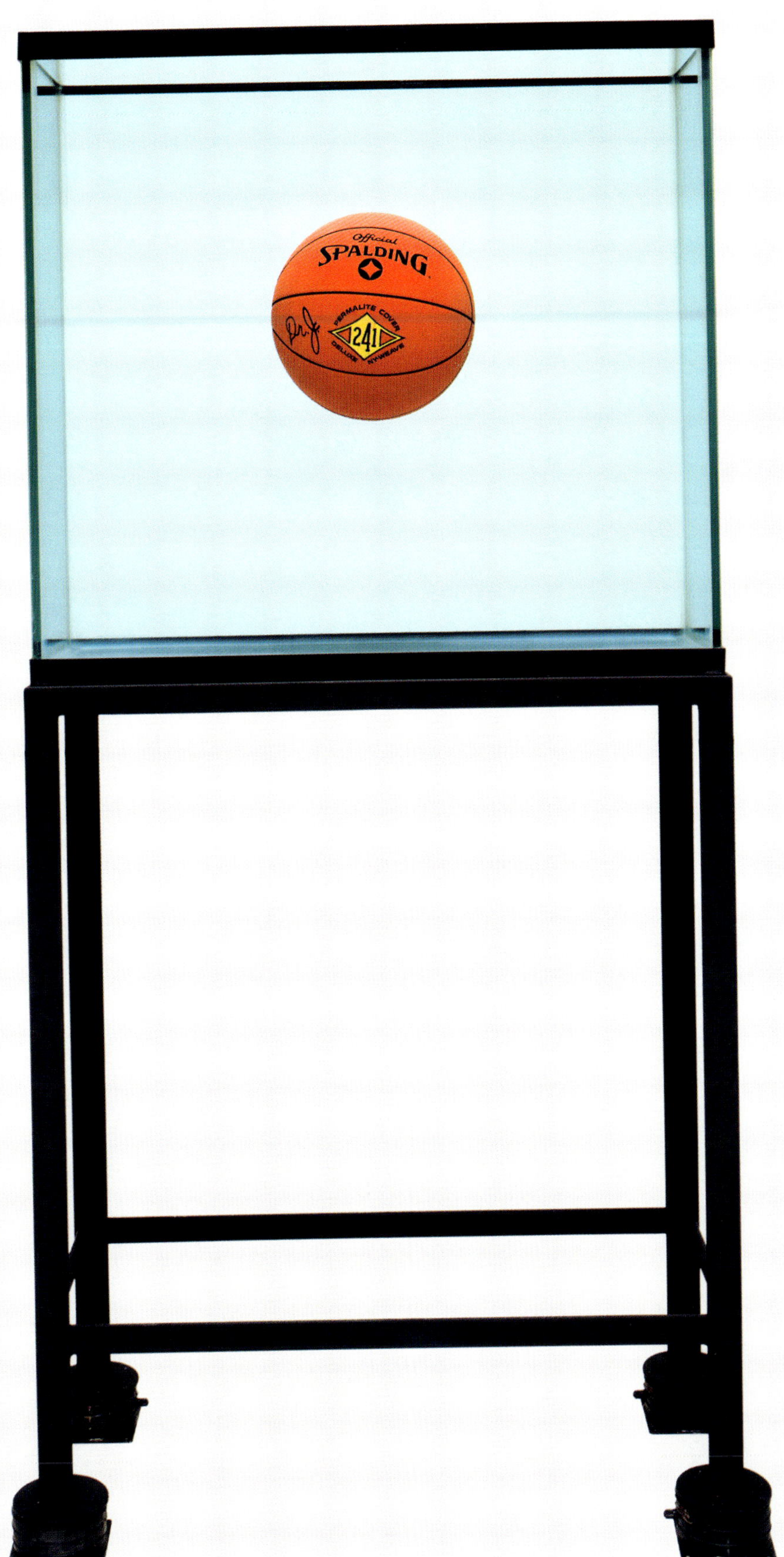
Official
SPALDING
PERMALITE COVER
241
DELUXE
NYWEAVE

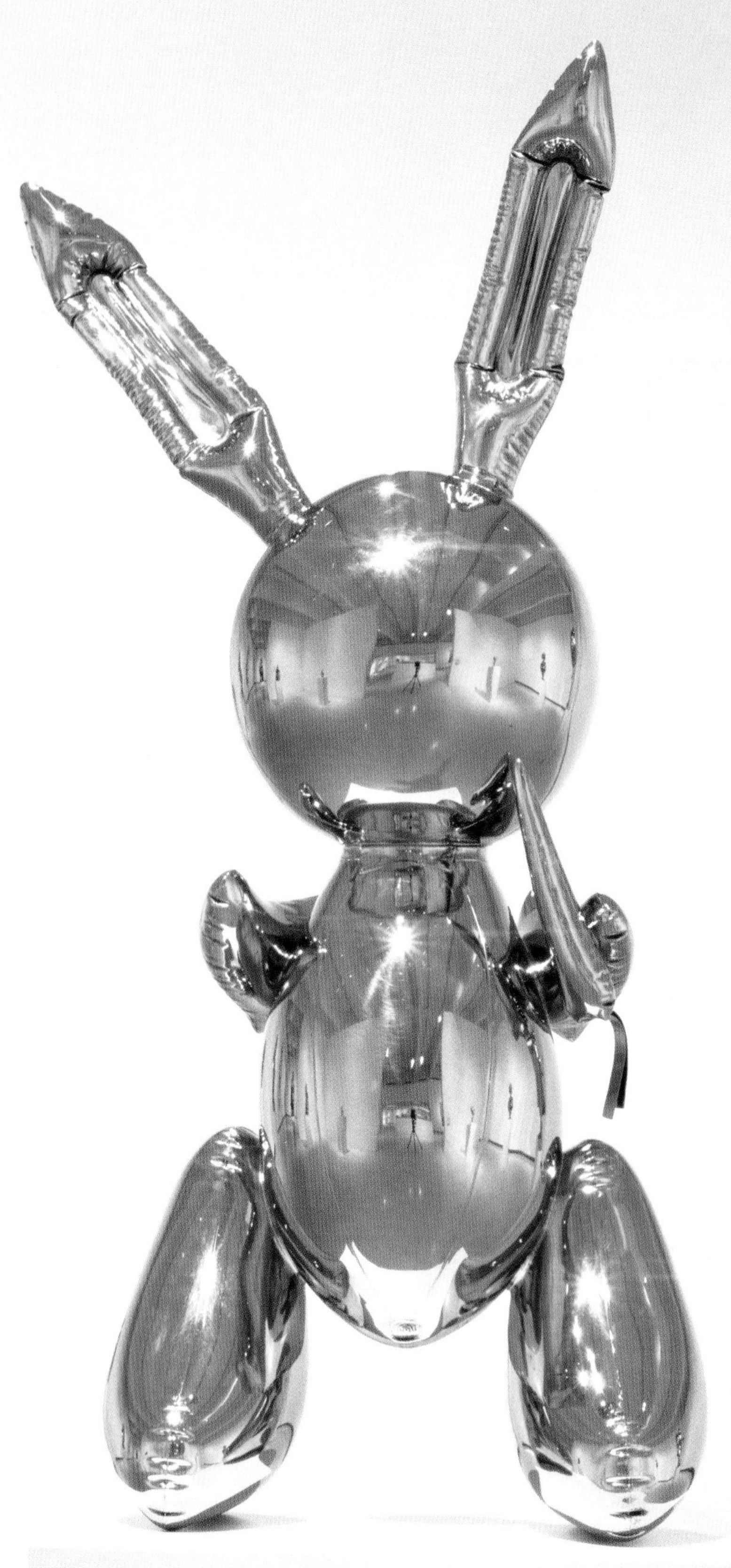

Rabbit

Cat. 2

My art has always used sex as a direct communication line to the viewer. The surface of my stainless steel pieces is pure sex and gives an object both a masculine and a feminine side: the weight of the steel engages with the femininity of the reflective surface.

Rabbit is one of the works that defines Koons for many people. Based on a 'ready-made', in this case an existing, cheap, inflatable toy, *Rabbit* is unexpectedly complex.

Part of the pleasure we derive from this piece (and giving pleasure is important to Koons) lies in the precision with which the steel imitates plastic. The puckers and seams of the original material keep trying to fool the brain. At the same time, Koons has modified the original to turn it into not just something else, but into many other things. Its scale gives *Rabbit* the gravitas of a classical or Renaissance sculpture. The disconcertingly blank face with its spherical head is a spaceman, or perhaps the Playboy logo. It is what each viewer brings to it - and the perfect sheen of the stainless steel surface means that viewers are always aware of themselves because of the multiple, distorted reflections in *Rabbit*'s curves.

— 1986
— Stainless steel
— 104.1 x 48.3 x 30.5 cm
— AP (and an edition of 3)
— The Eli and Edythe L. Broad Collection

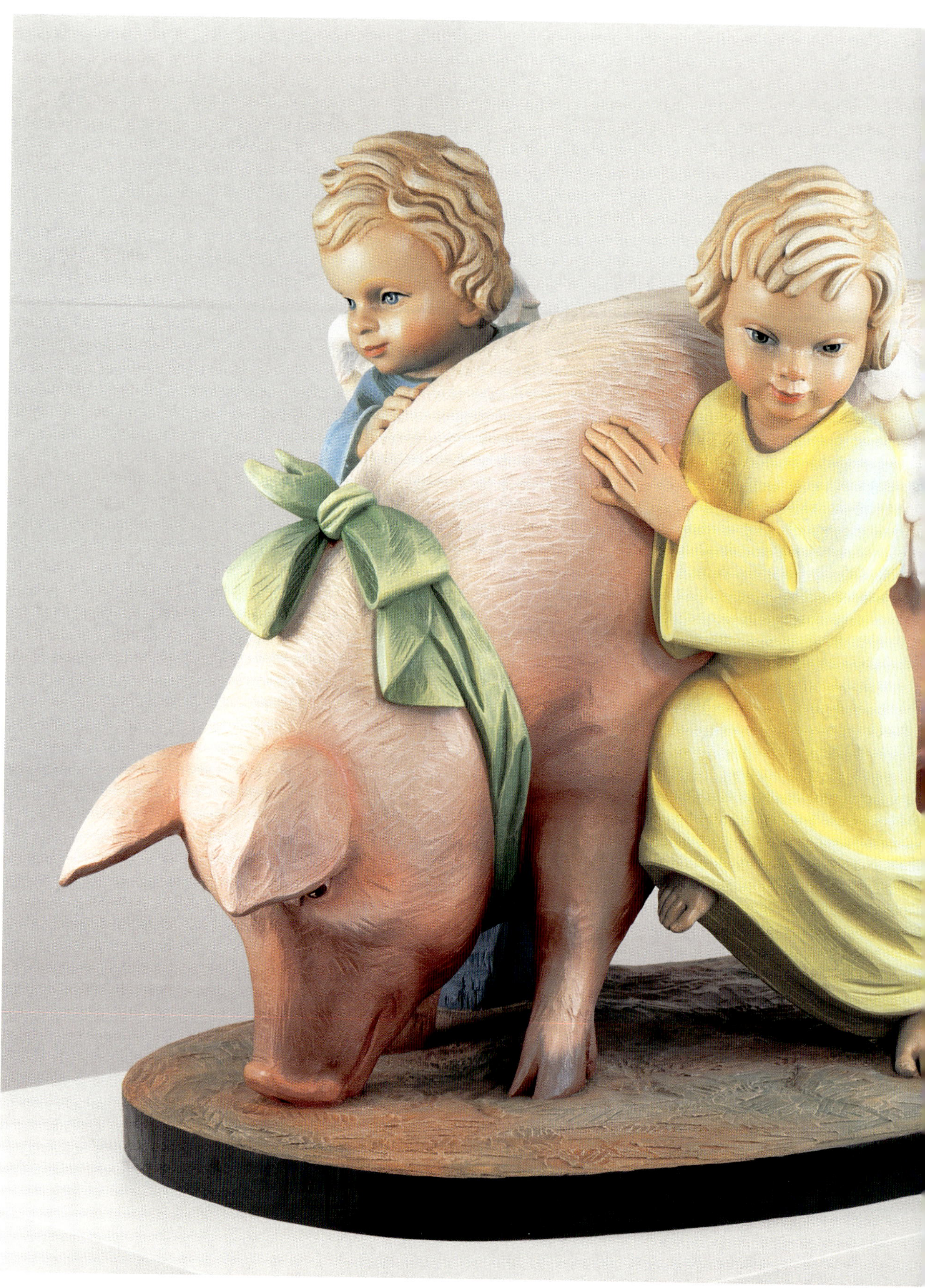

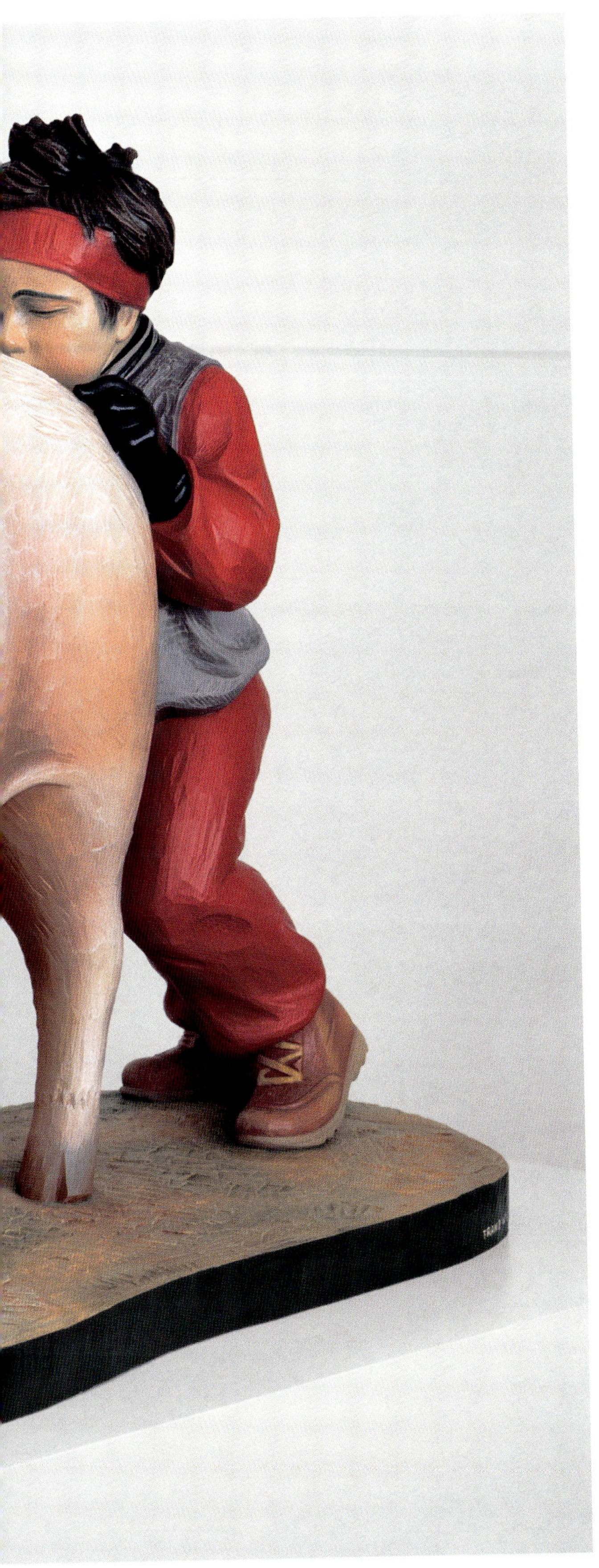

Ushering in Banality

Cat. 3

I wanted to make works that just embraced everyone's own cultural history and made everybody feel that their history was perfect just the way it was.

The *Banality* series re-imagined mass-produced trinkets and figurines on a hugely enlarged scale. They were meticulously crafted in porcelain or wood at specialist workshops in continental Europe. In this piece, the tracksuited boy pushing the pig from behind is Koons himself.

Koons's intention was to give people permission to love their cultural pasts, however lowbrow. Giving the cute and the kitsch the artistry and status of, say, a rococo sculpture encouraged people to stop feeling guilty about their guilty pleasures.

I used it to remove judgment and to remove the type of hierarchy that exists. I don't like to use the word 'kitsch' because kitsch is automatically making a judgement about something. I always saw 'banality' as a little freer than that.

I don't see a Hummel figurine as tasteless. I see it as beautiful. I see it and respond to the sentimentality in the work. I love the finish, how simple the colour green can be painted. I like things just being seen for what they are. It's like lying in the grass and taking a deep breath. That's all my work is trying to do, to be as enjoyable as that breath.

— 1988
— Polychromed wood
— 96.5 x 157.5 x 76.2 cm
— Edition 1 of an edition of 3 plus AP
— Private Collection

THE *ANTIQUITY* SERIES

Art is really just communication of something and the more archetypal it is, the more communicative it is.

In the *Antiquity* series Koons again explores favourite themes of breath, sexual desire and the blurring of distinctions between 'high' and 'low' art. This series draws upon antique and even prehistoric sculptures while also referencing other individual artworks – some famous, others with personal significance for the artist.

Antiquity 1

Cat. 4

I would hope that a viewer could come in and just get excited, as they would start to be visually stimulated from images. I would hope that it's very intuitive. It's not about using history or technique against the viewer.

The *Antiquity* series layers classical sculptures with elements from modern works which themselves also echo different periods of the past. Identifying the source of the individual elements is satisfying, but not, according to Koons, necessary. The images and their ideas are part of our shared cultural memory.

— 2009–12
— Oil on canvas
— 274.3 x 213.4 cm
— © Jeff Koons. Photo: Tom Powel Imaging
— Collection of the artist

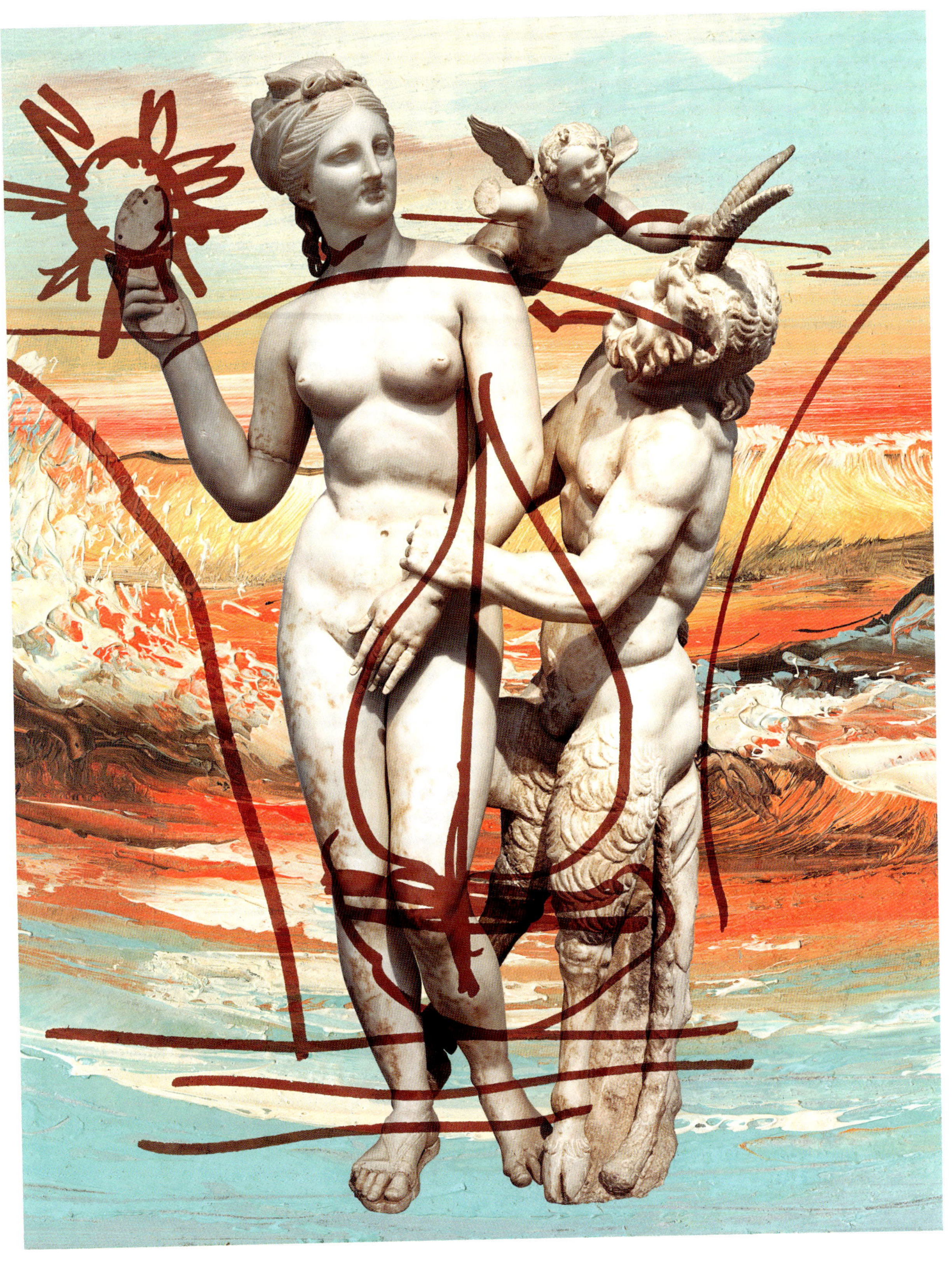

Antiquity 3

Cat. 5

At some point I realised that this monkey was really Eros and that Gretchen Mol was Aphrodite or Galatea. I actually found images of Aphrodite positioned on top of a dolphin with her son Eros, and I realised that this was the exact image that I had created.

To connect the present to the past is to continue to tie people to the narrative of biology. It is different from instinct but similar to instinct; we carry things with us in a very profound way, and this connecting force is a powerful narrative.

In 2006 Koons was asked to do a photo shoot for the *New York Times Magazine* with actress Gretchen Mol. She had just finished a film about Bettie Page, the 1950s pin-up girl described by Koons as 'the great American symbol of free sexuality'. Mol, in character as Page, was photographed by Koons with the inflatable dolphin and monkey. It was only afterwards that he discovered images of Aphrodite riding a dolphin. The connection was what inspired him to make the *Antiquity* series.

- 2009–11
- Oil on canvas
- 259.1 x 350.5 cm
- © Jeff Koons. Photo: Tom Powel Imaging
- Fundación Almine y Bernard Ruiz-Picasso para el Arte

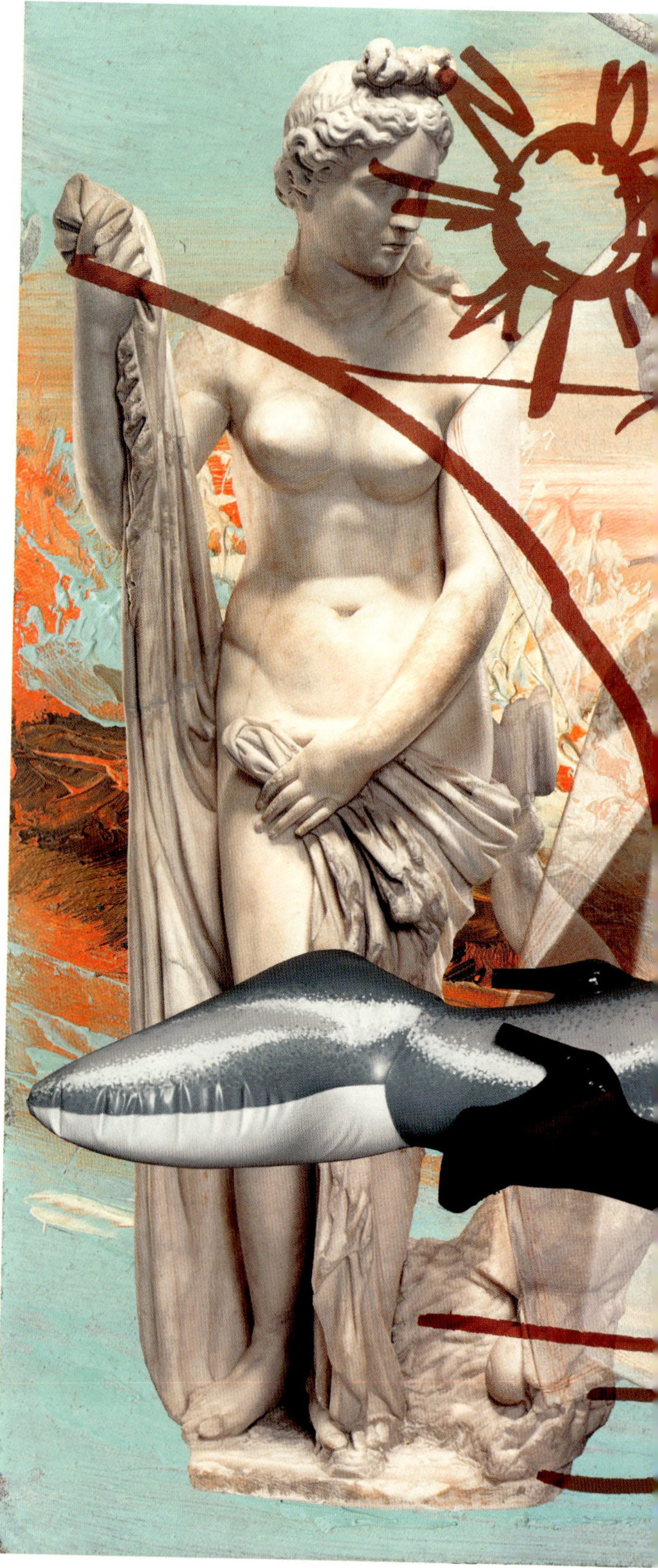

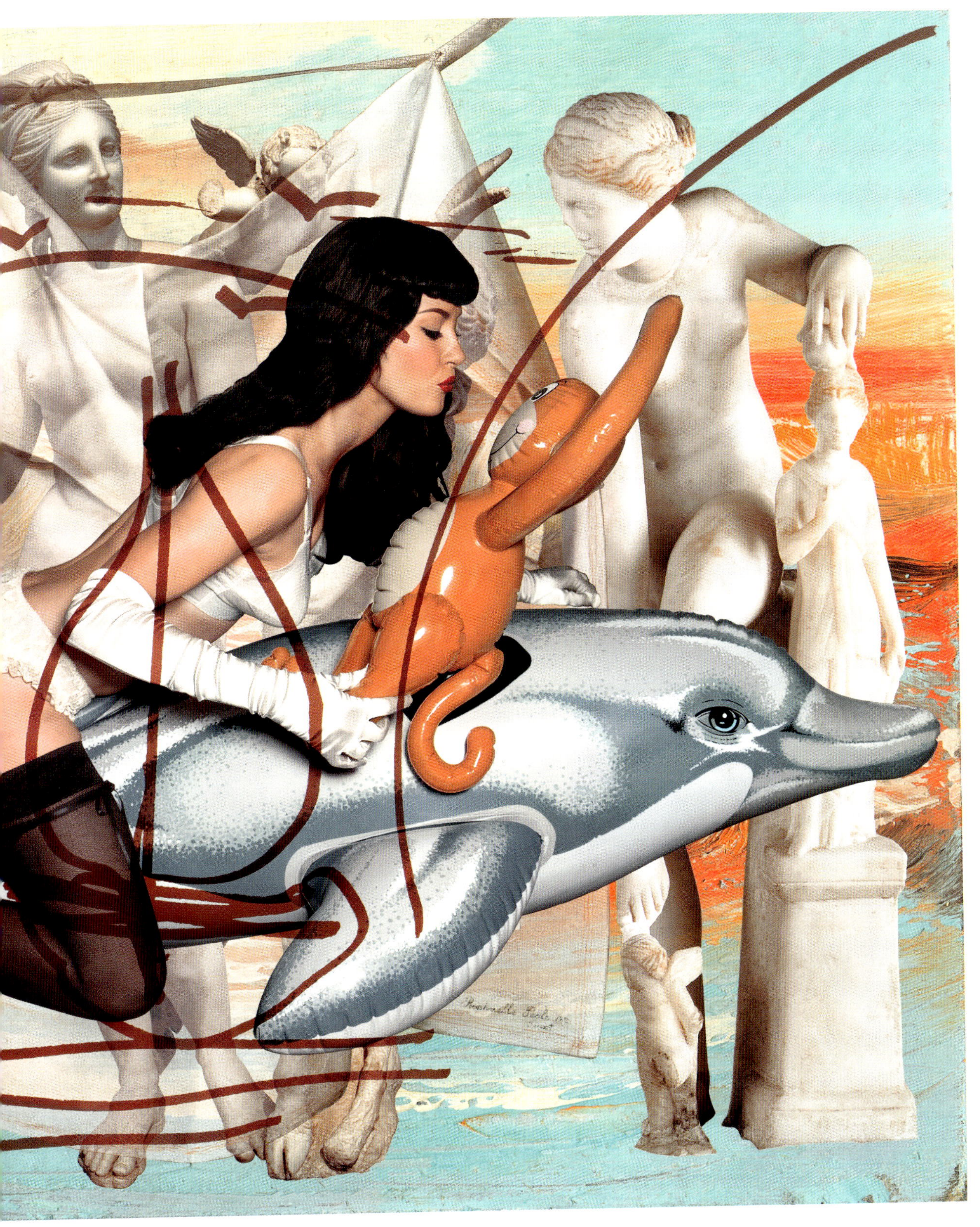

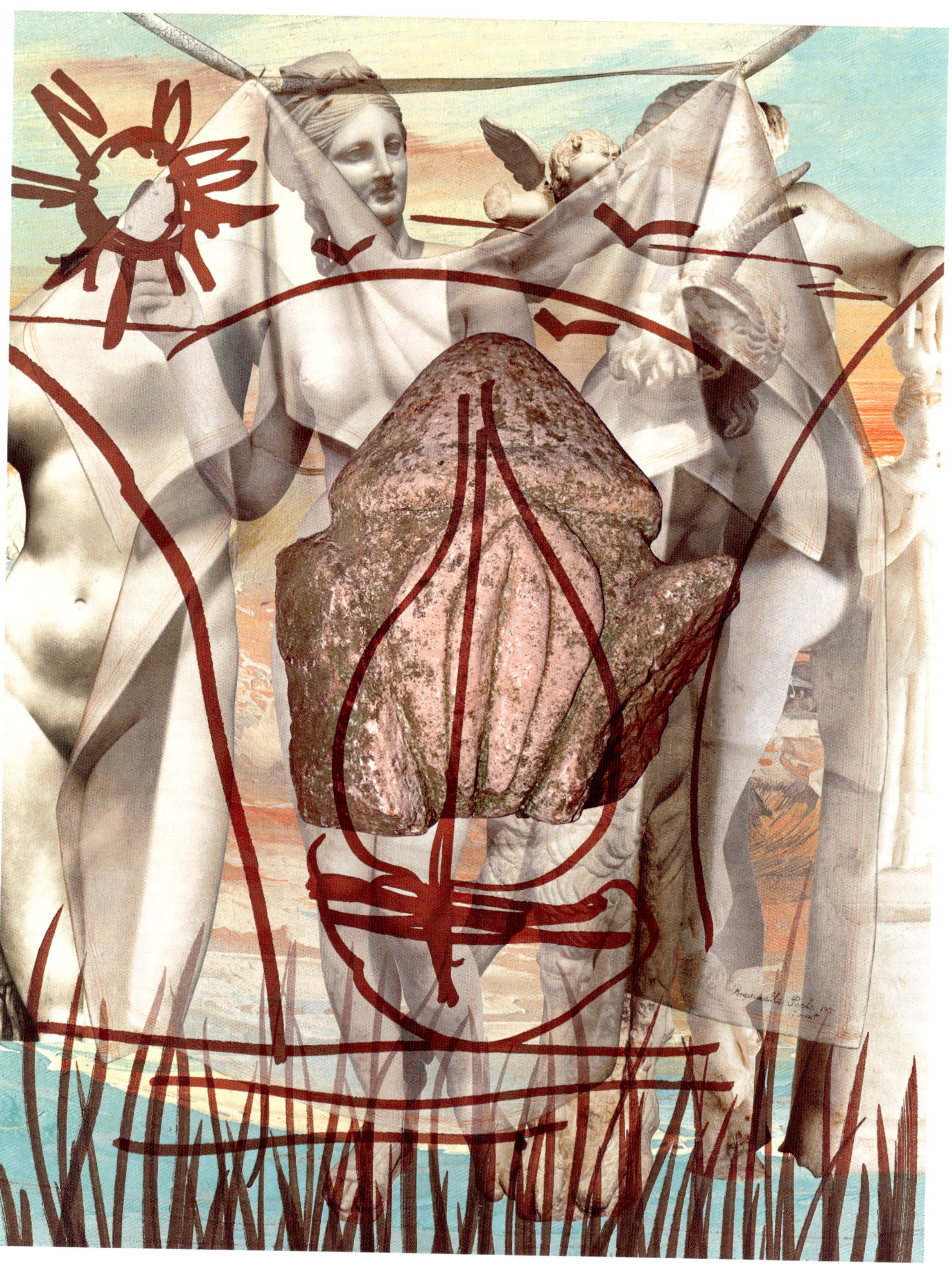

Antiquity 4
Cat. 6

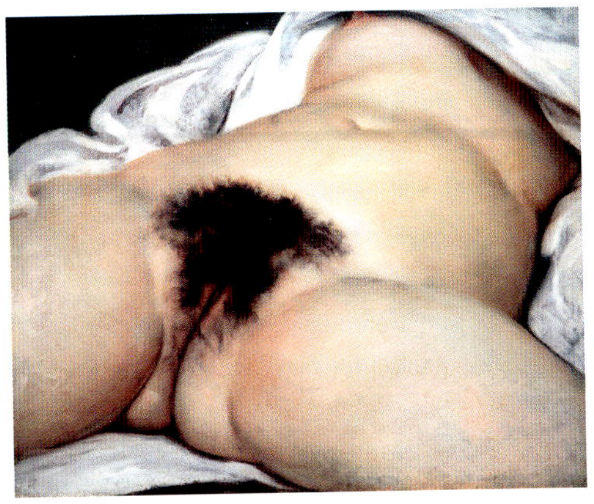

Gustave Courbet (1819–77)
The Origin of the World
***(L'Origine du monde)*, 1866**
Oil on canvas, 46 x 55 cm
PvE / Alamy Stock Photo

To know is an enrichment, but you don't have to; it's back to art not being an intimidating thing. You don't have to bring anything to it other than your own life experience because it's really about you and your interactions.

The ancient Greek sculptures in the background of the *Antiquity* paintings show Aphrodite, Eros and Pan. Aphrodite, goddess of love, brandishes a sandal at Pan as he tries to pull her hand away from her groin. The orange and blue background is taken from an oil painting of a seascape that Koons found lying in the street.

The bizarre object in front of them, made of up of both male and female genitalia, is a prehistoric sculpture that Koons bought off the internet. And on top of them – and all the *Antiquities* paintings – is the same scribbled sketch, based on a sort of visual *double entendre*: it is both a sailing boat with hills and a bright sun behind it and a 'hidden' image of a vagina, related by Koons to Courbet's famous painting *The Origin of the World.*

— 2010–13
— Oil on canvas
— 274.3 x 213.4 cm
— © Jeff Koons. Photo: Tom Powel Imaging
— Collection of the artist

Antiquity (Forest)

Cat. 7

I'm always interested to make a painting bigger than its parts, something that doesn't just seem to be composed by sticking things together. I want the connections to enrich the work and to hide the formal construction of the piece.

Each of the disparate elements in the *Antiquity* series is of personal significance to Koons. The background here is a copy of an early twentieth-century painting by the largely forgotten (and widely ridiculed) painter Eilshemius. Marcel Duchamp tried to champion him, however, and Koons is also a huge fan.

Integrating classical Greek sculpture into his work was a departure from the lowbrow subjects of his earlier pieces. It creates a dialogue between past and present that is told in a much more conventional way in the Ashmolean's permanent collection. Koons is tapping into a shared cultural past that is, consciously or unconsciously, an integral part of our make-up – even part of our biology, according to the artist.

— 2010–13
— Oil on canvas
— 274.3 x 213.4 cm
— © Jeff Koons. Photo: Tom Powel Imaging
— Stefan T. Edlis Collection

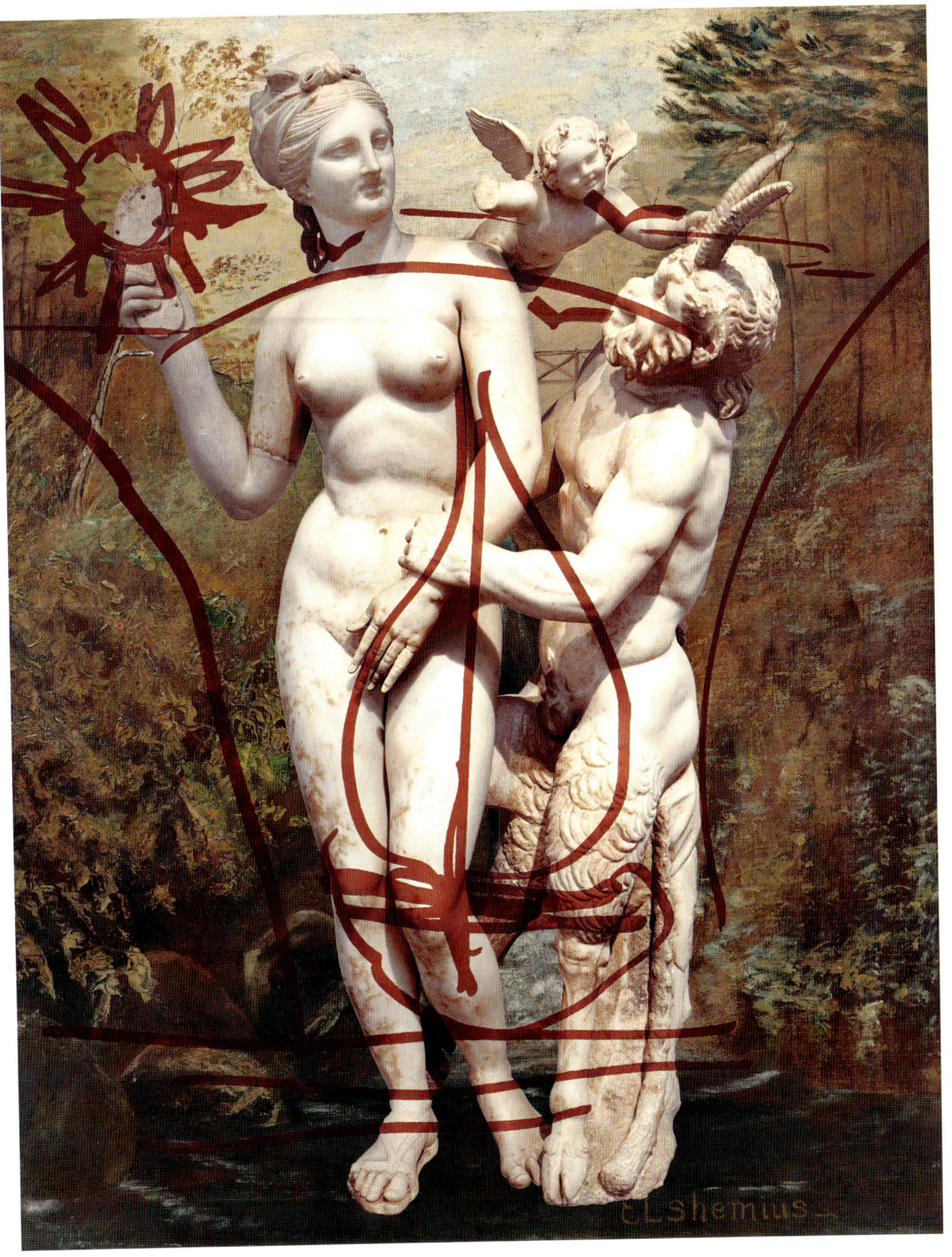
ELshemius

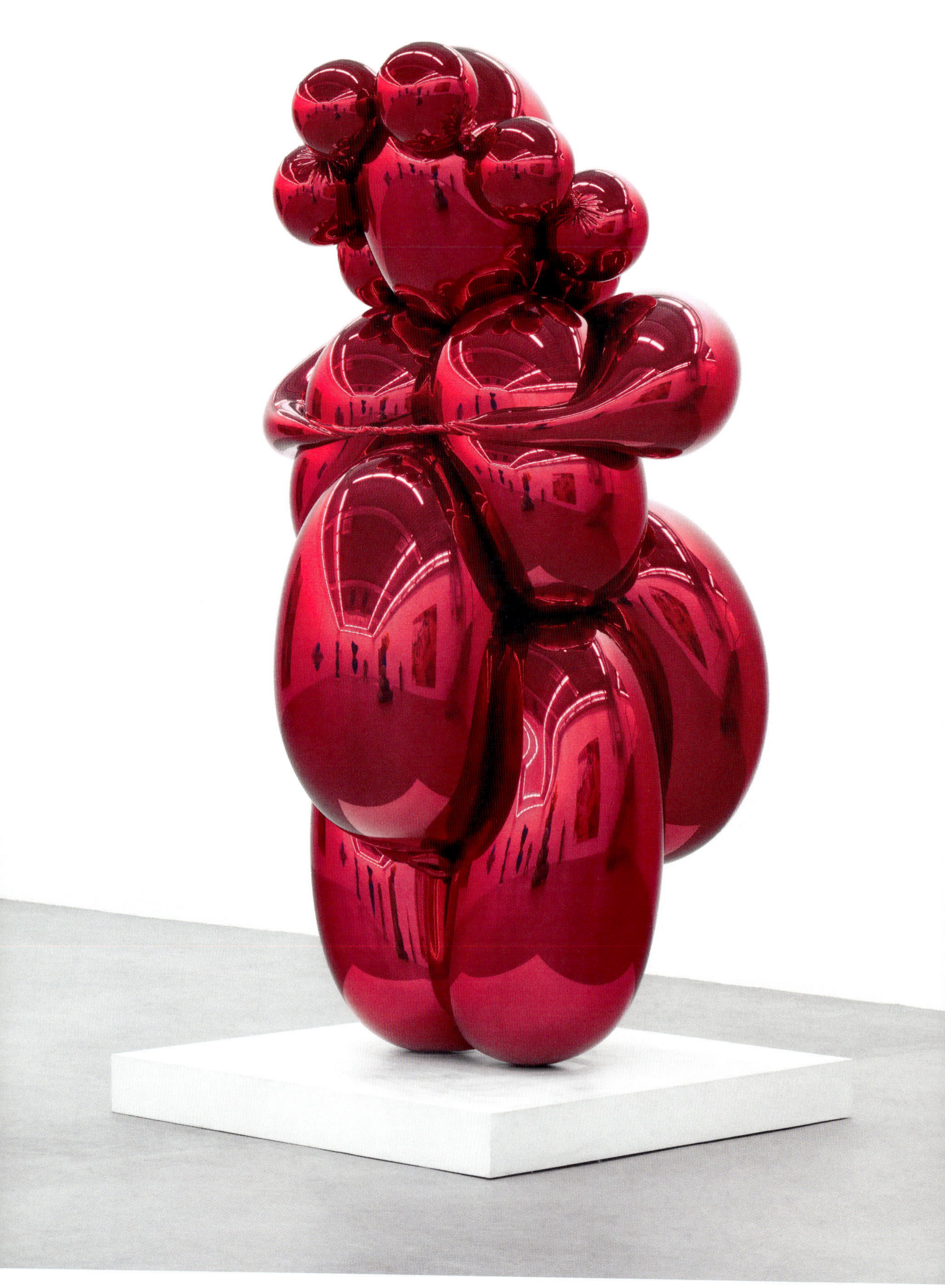

Balloon Venus (Magenta)
Cat. 8

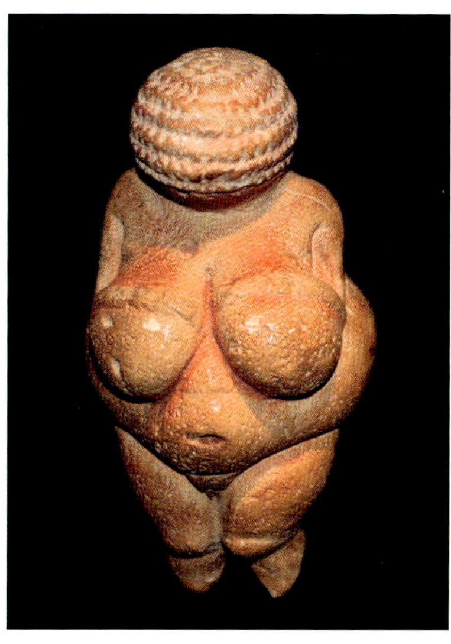

Venus of Willendorf
Late Paleolithic stone statuette, Austria, 24,000–22,000 BC.
World History Archive / Alamy Stock Photo

To connect the present to the past is to continue to tie people to the narrative of biology. It is different from instinct but similar to instinct; we carry things with us in a very profound way, and this connecting force is a powerful narrative.

Balloon Venus (Magenta) is inspired by a tiny Stone Age fertility figure known as the *Venus of Willendorf*. Koons has put this figure through a double transformation: from limestone sculpture to balloon model, and from balloons to his trademark, super-reflective, coloured steel on a huge scale. The artist insisted on the model being made from a single balloon to maximise the sense of a continuous pressure all over. Instead of simply making a 3D scan of the model, he used an industrial CT scanner to produce minutely detailed information that could be further manipulated on a computer.

The vast finished figure, nearly 1.5 tons in weight, is 'a symbol of life energy'. For Koons she has the energy of a cult figure, an ancient tribal goddess - but conceived in materials that also place her firmly in the present.

— 2008–12
— Mirror-polished stainless steel with transparent colour coating
— 259.1 x 121.9 x 127 cm
— One of five unique versions
— © Jeff Koons. Photo: Marc Domage. Courtesy Almine Rech Gallery
— The Broad Art Foundation, Los Angeles

Ballerinas
Cat. 9

I might be able to find something anywhere, at any moment, that I could somehow make art out of in some way, enrich it or connect it to something else and embed it with more vitality. So I'm consciously always involved in that activity.

The startling transformation of something tiny and fragile into something immense and indestructible has become a trademark Koonsian theme. He transformed a decorative porcelain figurine of two dancers into an abstract symbol of transcendence through subtle colour gradations and its grand scale. The relationship of the two figures echoes that of the Venus and satyr in Koons's contemporary series of *Antiquity* paintings.

— 2010–14
— Mirror-polished stainless steel with transparent colour coating
— 254 x 177.8 x 157.5 cm
— Edition 3 of an edition of 3 plus AP
— © Jeff Koons. Photos: Fredrik Nilsen, 2017. Courtesy Gagosian
— The Broad Art Foundation, Los Angeles

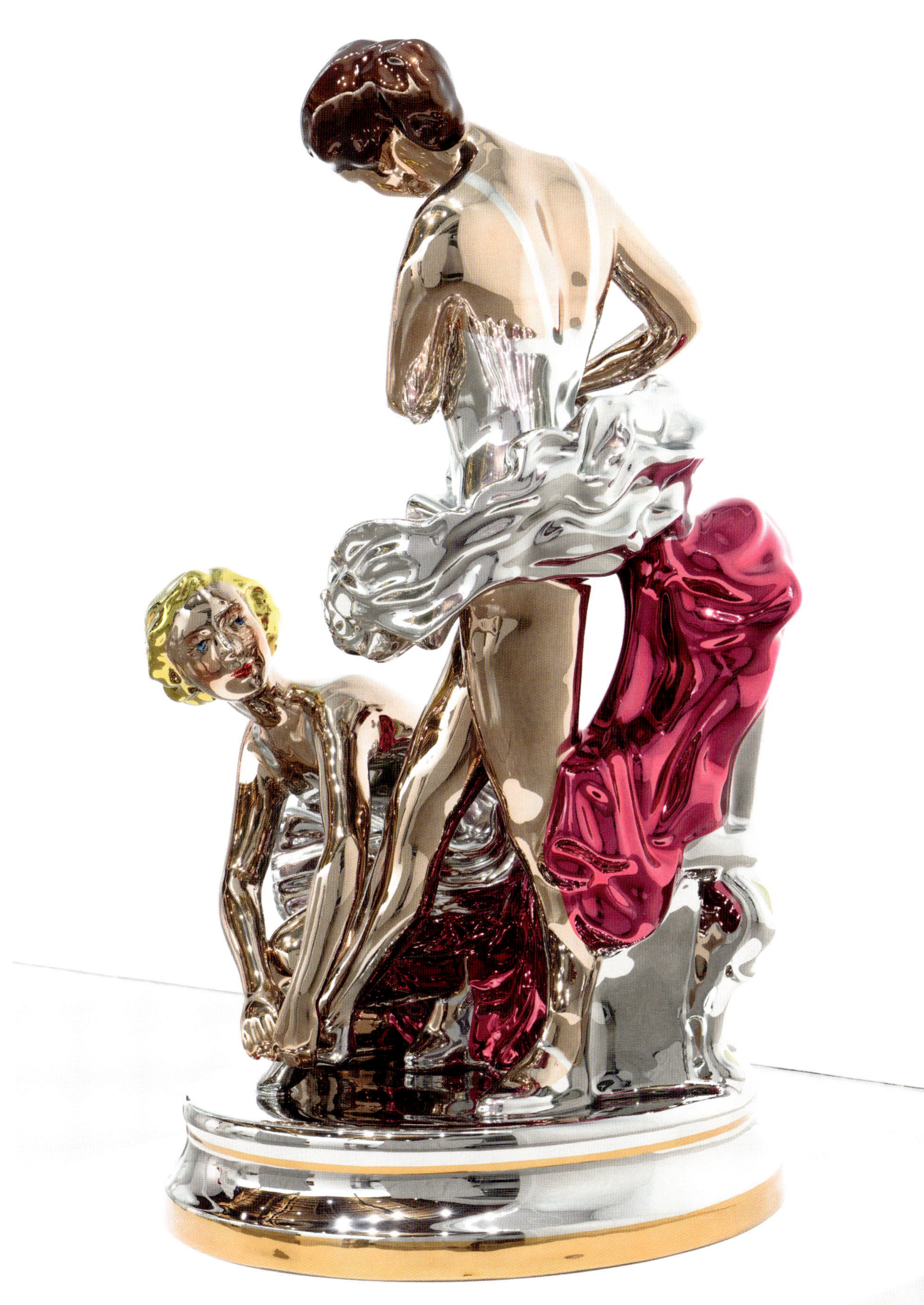

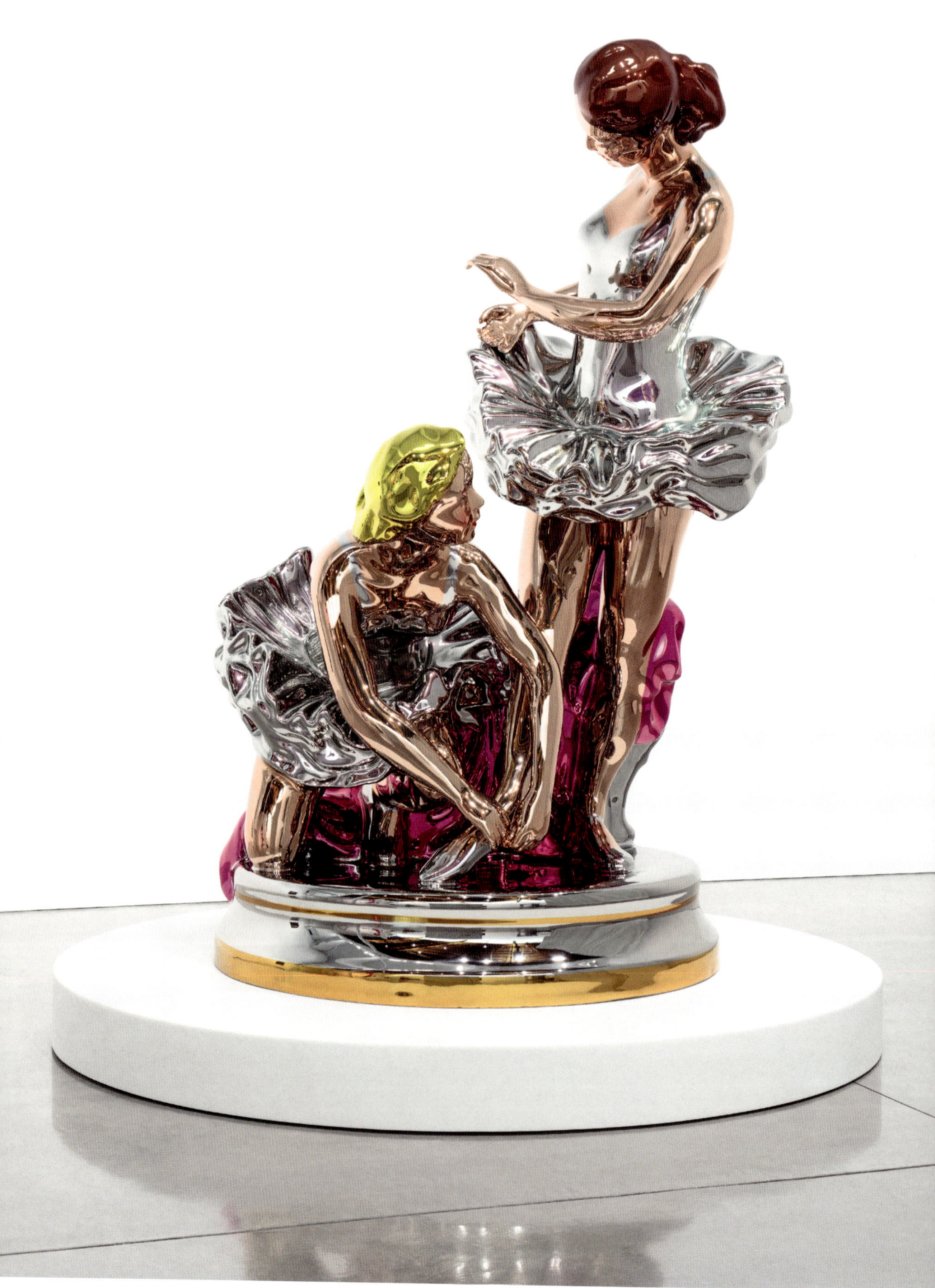

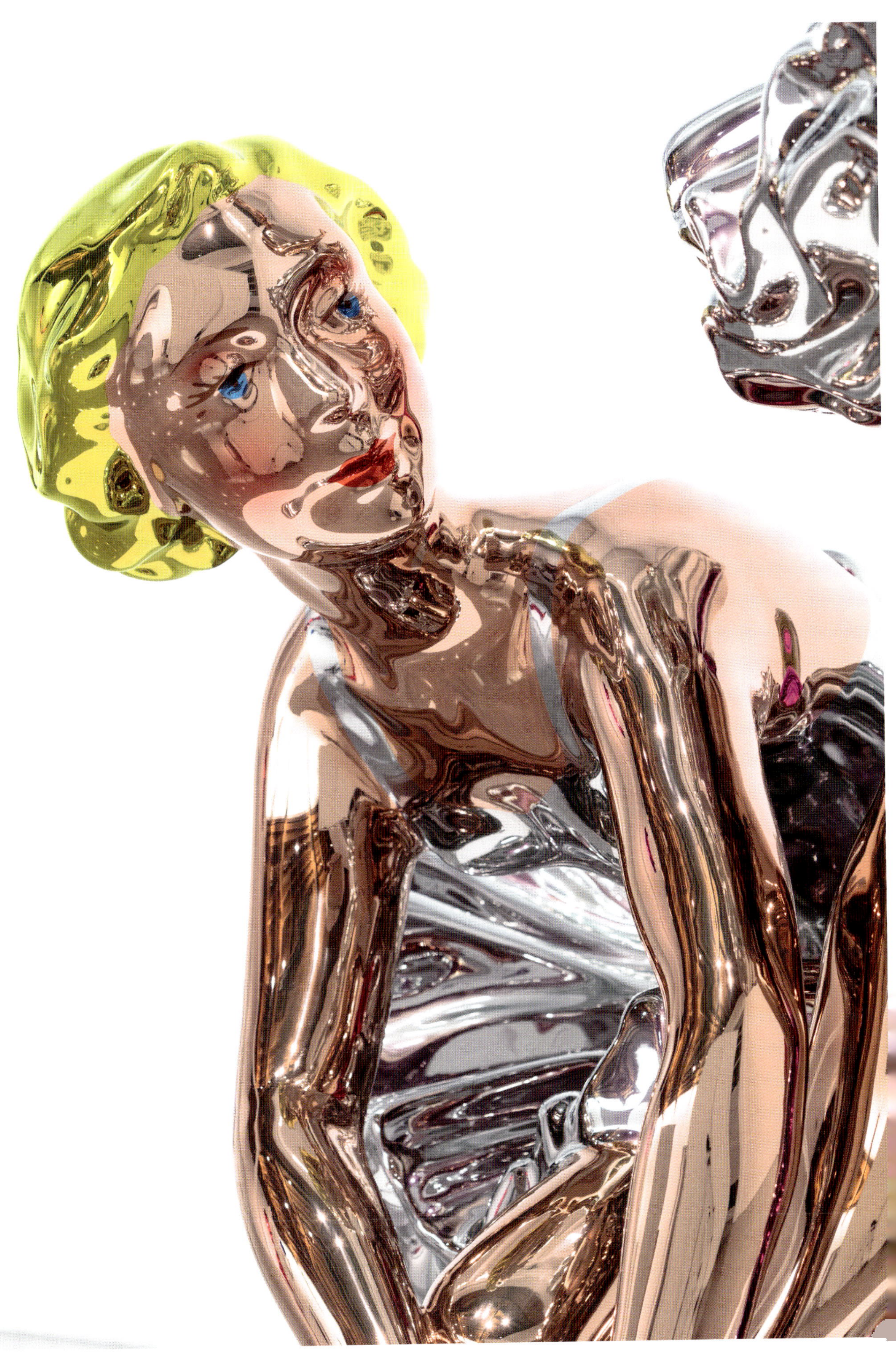

Seated Ballerina

Cat. 10

Seated Ballerina *is like a Venus. You could be looking at a* Venus of Willendorf *or some of the oldest Venuses. It is really about beauty and even a sense of contemplation, a sense of ease.*

It is hard not to see Koons's work as ironic, but he insists it is not: 'Irony causes too much critical contemplation.' His *Seated Ballerina* is taken from an Eastern European porcelain figurine, but reproduced on the scale of a monumental sculpture in reflective stainlesss steel with transparent colour coating. Her pose echoes that of a classical crouching Venus; the work also references Degas's sculptures and images of ballet dancers at rest.

I've tried to make work that any viewer, no matter where they came from, would have to respond to, would have to say that on some level 'Yes, I like it'. If they couldn't do that, it would only be because they had been told they were not supposed to like it. Eventually they will be able to strip all that down and say: 'You know it's silly, but I like that piece. It's great.'

— 2010–15
— Mirror-polished stainless steel with transparent colour coating
— 210.8 x 113.5 x 199.8 cm
— Artist's proof of an edition of 3 plus AP
—
— Collection of the artist

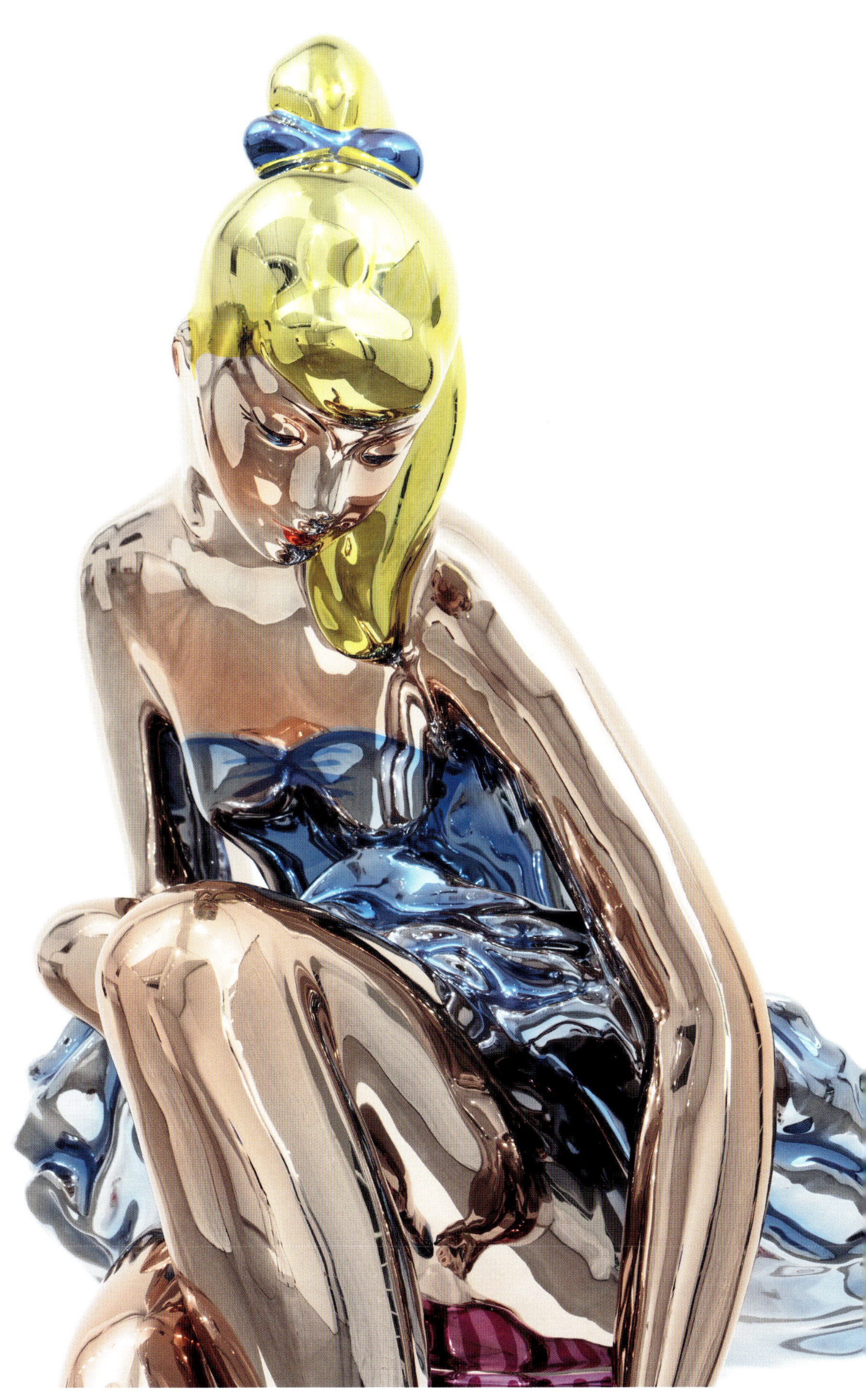

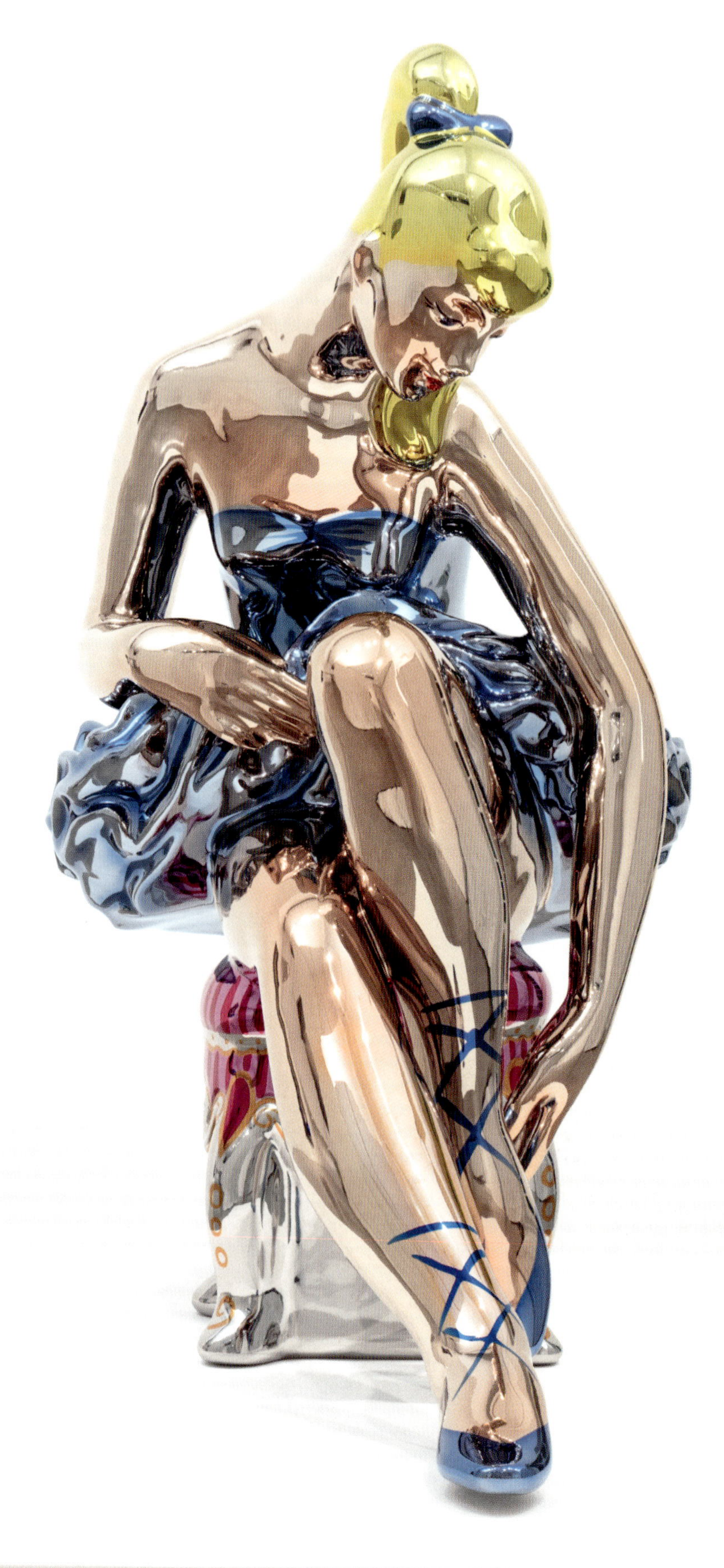

Gazing Ball (Birdbath)

Cat. 11

The truest narrative we have of human history is in our genes, in our DNA. And so this type of linkage that exists internally within our biology also exists externally and I wanted to manifest that, to bring it out into reality.

In the *Gazing Ball* series both viewer and artwork are included in the balls' reflections, whereas Koons's earlier statues showed just the viewer in their reflective surfaces. Here he deliberately chooses iconic works from Western art, especially paintings that both refer back to earlier works and have inspired later artists. The series thus affirms our place in the past, present and future.

Koons's versions of old masters are meticulously reproduced but not intended to be exact copies. He changes scale and the brushstrokes do not echo the texture of the original work: 'They are just the idea of the painting,' Koons explains. Yet his workshop assistants meticulously apply each brushstroke by hand, using a print out of a digital image as a reference. Casts receive the same attention to detail, uniting elements of different surviving casts with reference to the original sculptures.

Each glass ball that features in the series is hand-blown; around 350 are rejected for every one sufficiently flawless to feature in a work.

When I grew up, if you drove through Pennsylvania, people would put gazing balls in front of their houses. There's a kind of generosity about that. Your neighbour doesn't have to do that for you, they do that for whoever drives by.

Reflective gazing balls are usually sold in suburban American garden centres, along with birdbaths and water features. The versions that Koons uses are handmade, specifically for him. Koons's preoccupation with them ties in with recurring themes in his work: breath (they are hollow and hand-blown) and the presence of the viewer in the artwork – it is impossible to look at a gazing ball without also seeing yourself and your surroundings. For Koons the gazing ball 'represents the vastness of the universe and at the same time the intimacy of right here, right now'.

— 2013
— Plaster and glass
— 114.9 x 69.9 x 69.9 cm
— Artist's proof of an edition of 3 plus AP
— © Jeff Koons. Photo: Tom Powel Imaging. Courtesy Gagosian
— Collection of the artist

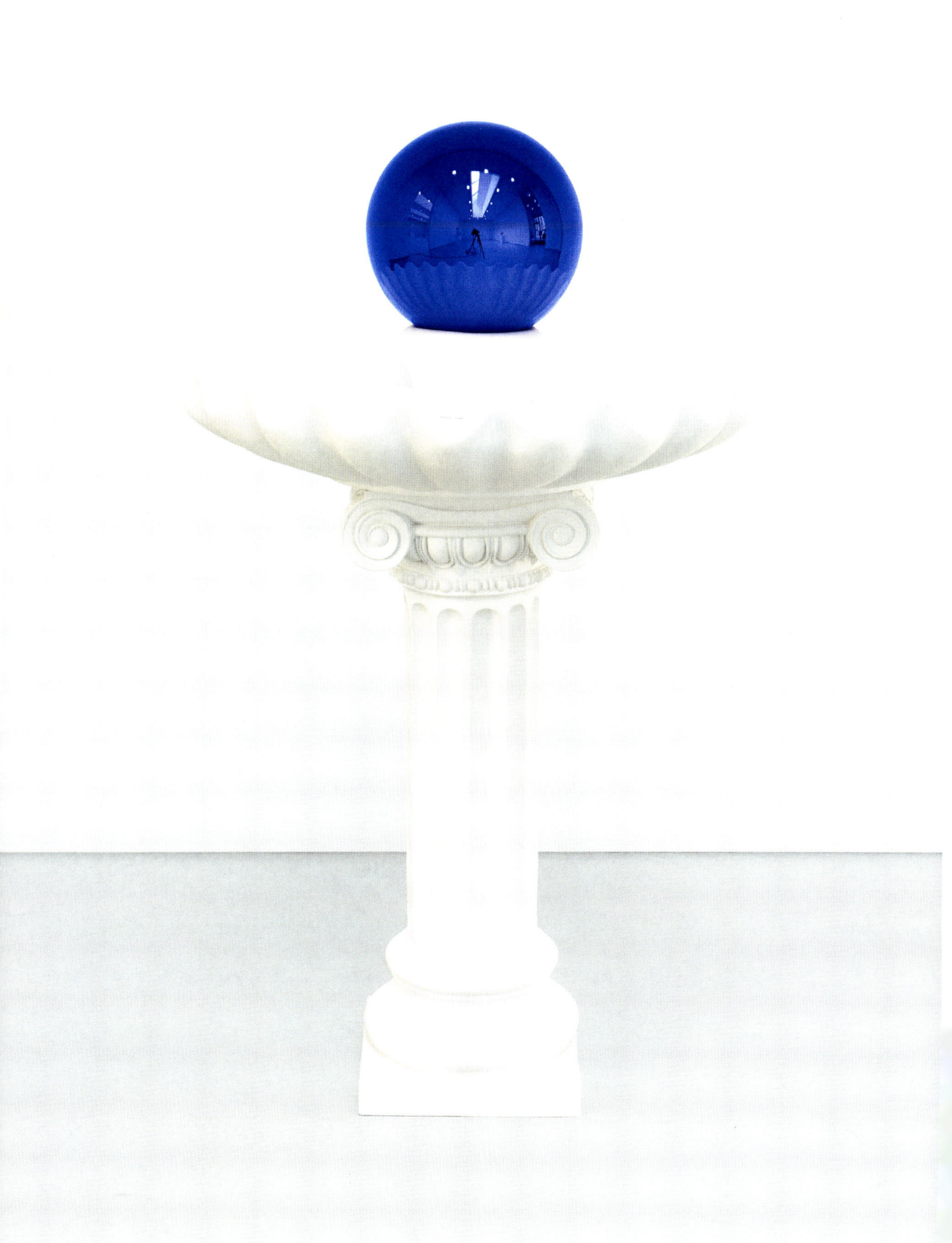

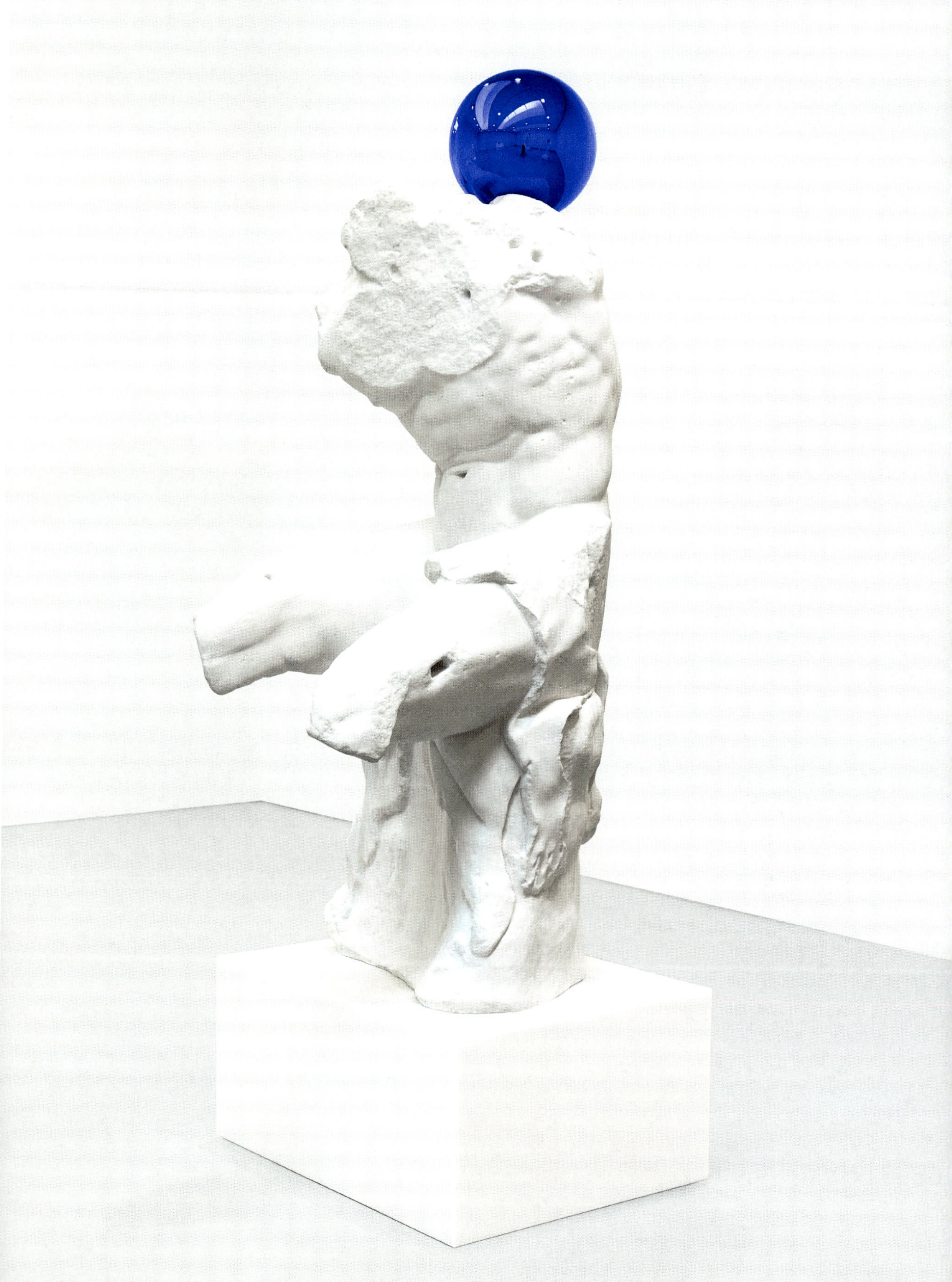

Gazing Ball (Belvedere Torso)

Cat. 12

People are going to have their own perceptions. They will look at things differently. I think looking at art, the way people respond to it, gives a kind of view into how open people are to the world around them. And if they're closed about really exposing themselves to a painting or to a sculpture, then you can imagine they're probably relative closed to other experiences.

The muscular *Belvedere Torso* is an ancient Greek sculpture and probably the most reproduced classical sculpture in history. The original work is in the Vatican, but casts of it - and casts of casts - can be found all over Europe. Generations of art students have had to draw the sculpture as part of their training, from Michelangelo to the present.

— 2013
— Plaster and glass
— 181.6 x 75.9 x 89.2 cm
— Artist's proof of an edition of 3 plus AP
— © Jeff Koons. Photo: Tom Powel Imaging. Courtesy Gagosian
— Collection of the artist

Gazing Ball (Silenus with Baby Dionysus)
Cat. 13

Reflection affirms the viewer. It affirms the right here, right now, and from that point you can start to time travel. You can play with metaphysics.

In Greek mythology Silenus was a satyr who became tutor and companion to Dionysus, god of wine. This statue - or copies of it - have multiplied across the world over the 2000 years since it was created, supposedly by Praxiteles, the greatest of classical Greek sculptors. Several copies were made in Roman times and casts of the work have proliferated over the centuries. Today Silenus can be spotted in galleries and parks all over Europe and the United States.

— 2013
— Plaster and glass
— 202.2 x 86.4 x 85.4 cm
— Artist's proof of an edition of 3 plus AP
— © Jeff Koons. Photo: Tom Powel Imaging. Courtesy Gagosian
— Collection of the artist

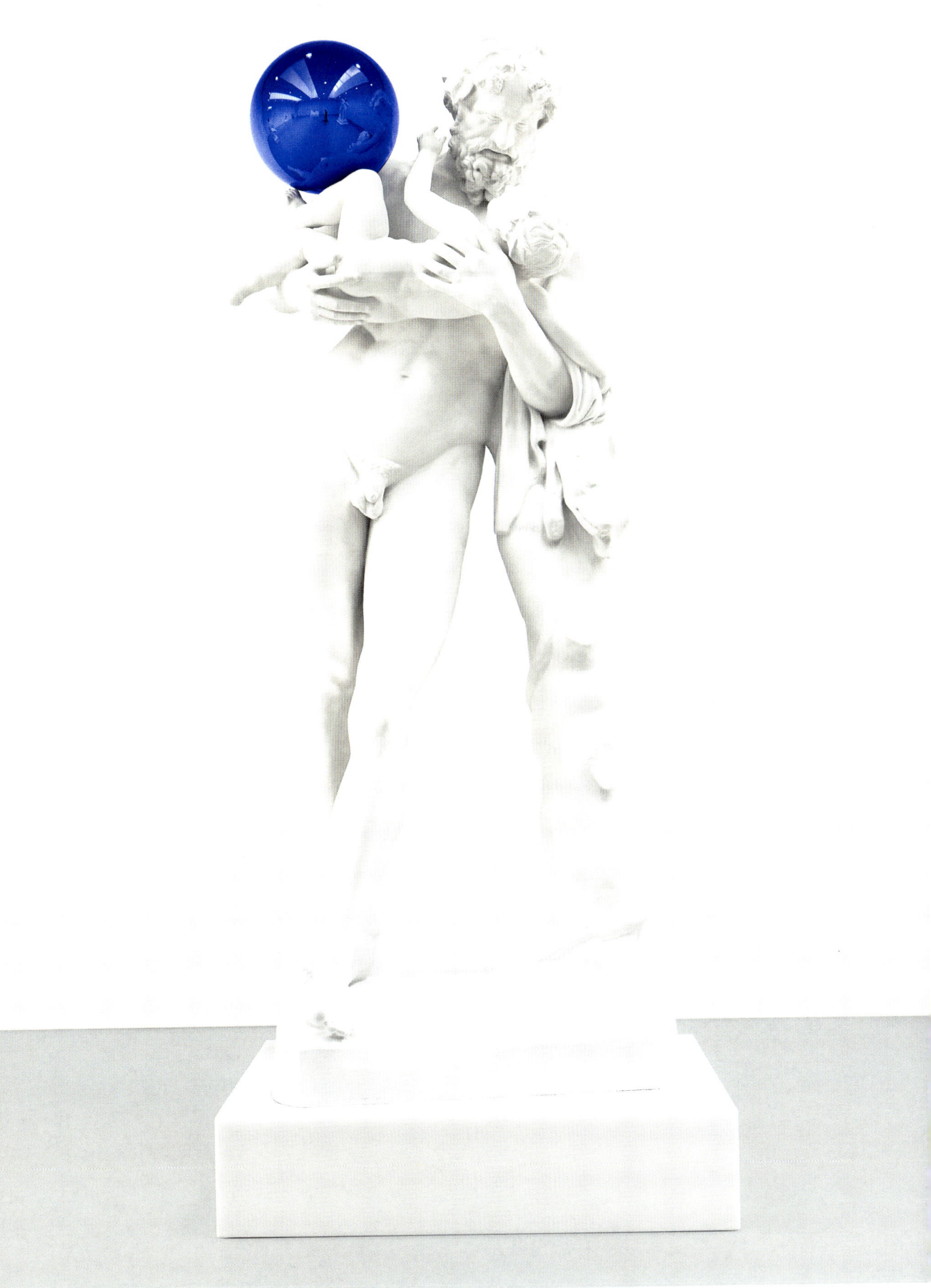

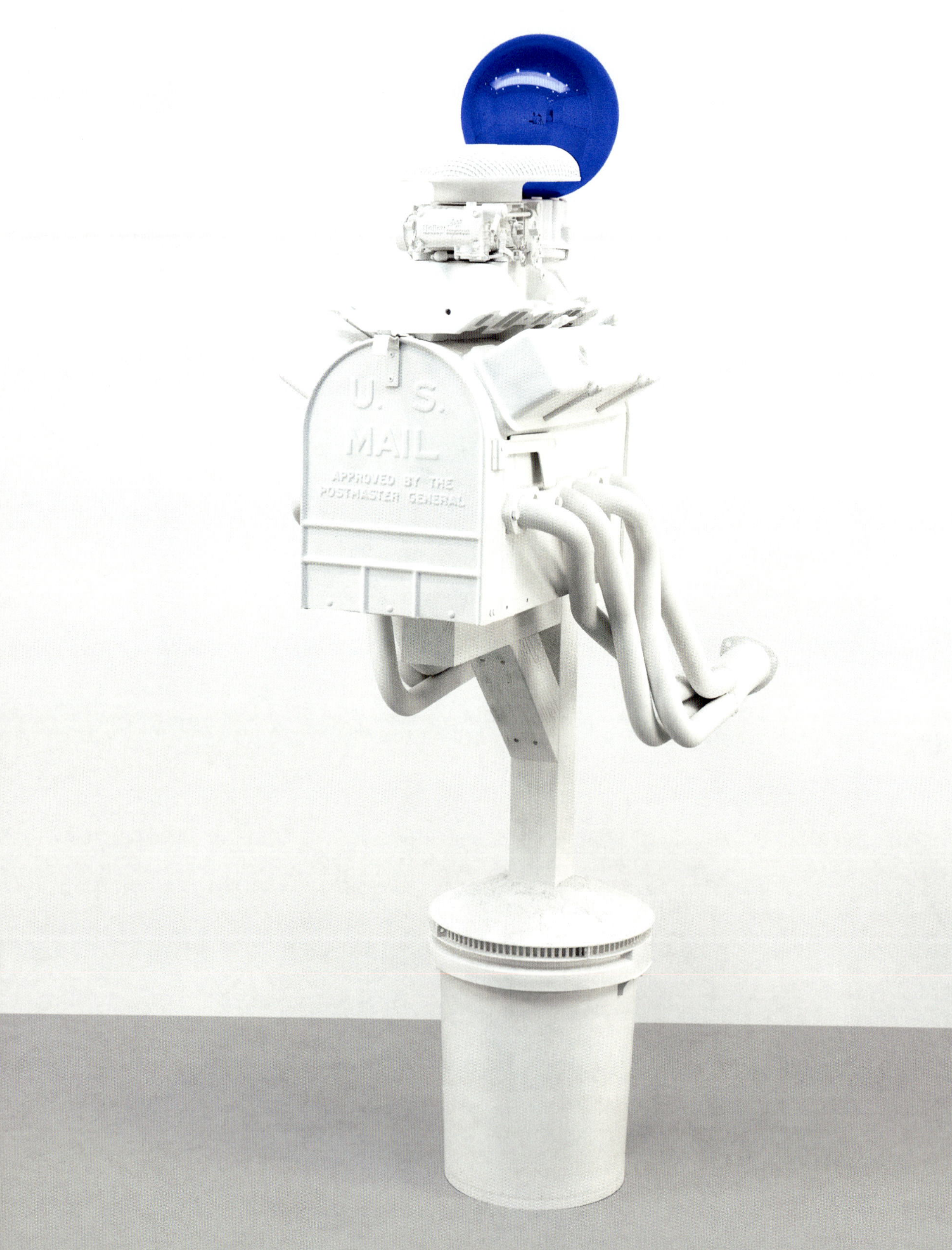
U. S.
MAIL
APPROVED BY THE
POSTMASTER GENERAL

Gazing Ball (Mailbox)

Cat. 14

It's a GPS system. Because it reflects almost 360 degrees and it tells you everything it can about where you are in the universe. Your brain is always secreting chemicals because it wants to know where you are in the universe.

The mailbox Koons has used is the characteristically American type that is detached from the house, freestanding on a pole (in this case planted in a plastic bucket). At the same time the artist has amalgamated the mailbox with with parts of a automobile engine as one may encounter in the rural American landscape. The entire object is vaguely masculine, and it creates a narrative about one's self, community and the external world.

— 2013
— Plaster and glass
— 188.6 x 61.9 x 105.4 cm
— Artist's proof of an edition of 3 plus AP
— © Jeff Koons. Photo: Tom Powel Imaging. Courtesy David Zwirner
— Collection of the artist

Gazing Ball (Titian Diana and Actaeon)
Cat. 15

If I look at a Titian painting or you look at Leonardo's painting, you first have sensations, you have feelings, and then it leads to the development of ideas – to the intellect.

Painted in the 1550s for the king of Spain, Titian portrays Actaeon accidentally stumbling on the secret bathing place of Diana, goddess of hunting. Her revenge was to turn him into a stag to be hunted to death by his own hounds: the stag's skull at the top right serves to remind the viewer of what happened next.

Titian's spontaneous method is the opposite of Koons's meticulous technique. Titian's energetic brushwork is visible, but the surface of Koons's painting painstakingly reproduces the appearance – rather than the texture – of the work's original, free-flowing brushstrokes.

— 2014–15
— Oil on canvas, glass and aluminium
— 173 x 188 x 37.5 cm
— © Jeff Koons. Photo: Tom Powel Imaging. Courtesy Gagosian
— Collection of the artist

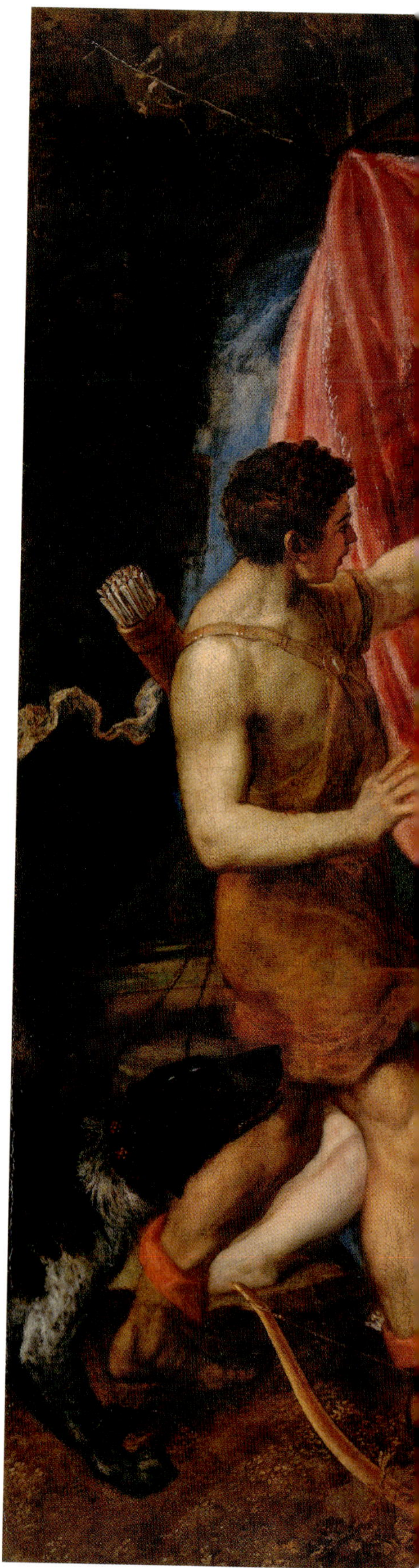

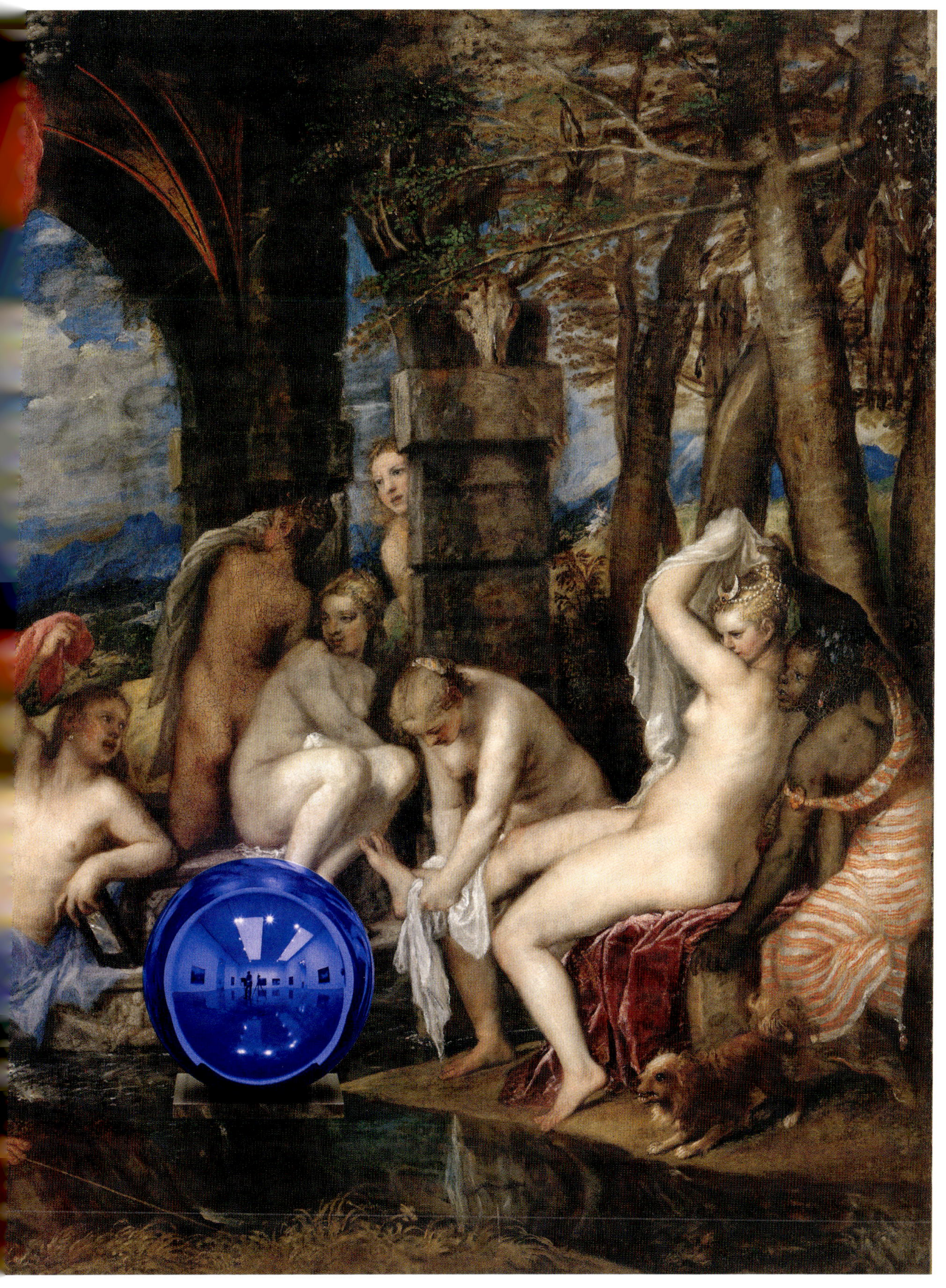

Gazing Ball (Rubens Tiger Hunt)
Cat. 16

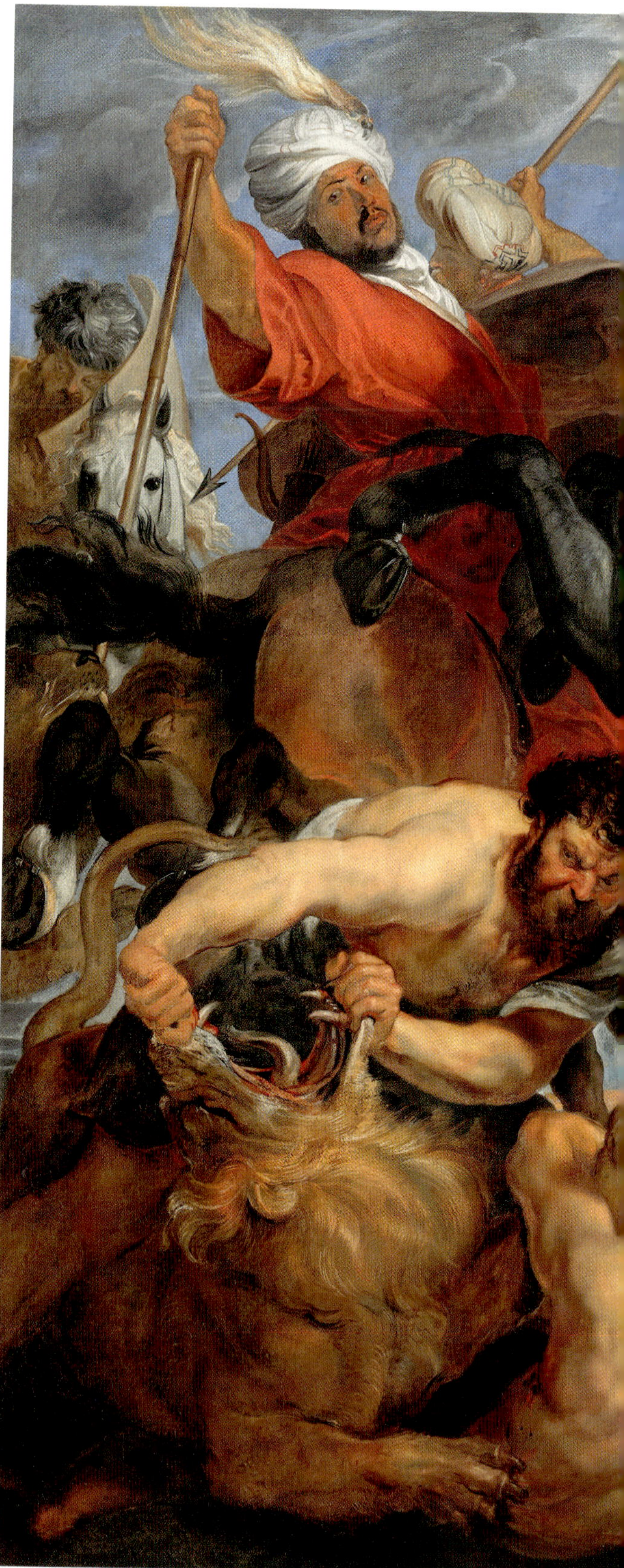

I love to make reference to other artists – kind of art about art in that it's a way to time travel, to pay homage to our forebears. Everything – all the information, all the knowledge, everything that has been brought to the table to this moment.

Peter Paul Rubens painted *The Tiger Hunt* in 1615–16 in his studio in Antwerp. The original is even bigger, almost life-sized. In Koons's work the gazing ball covers up the view through to a bright, blue seascape; the world behind the action is replaced with the world in front of it.

Rubens was Flemish but had travelled in Spain and Italy, absorbing the influence of the Renaissance masters. *The Tiger Hunt* draws directly on a painting by Leonardo da Vinci. Rubens also made a copy of Titian's *Diana and Actaeon* which Koons also included in his *Gazing Ball* series.

— 2015
— Oil on canvas, glass and aluminium
— 163.8 x 211.1 x 37.5 cm
— © Jeff Koons. Photo: Tom Powel Imaging. Courtesy Gagosian
— Collection of the artist

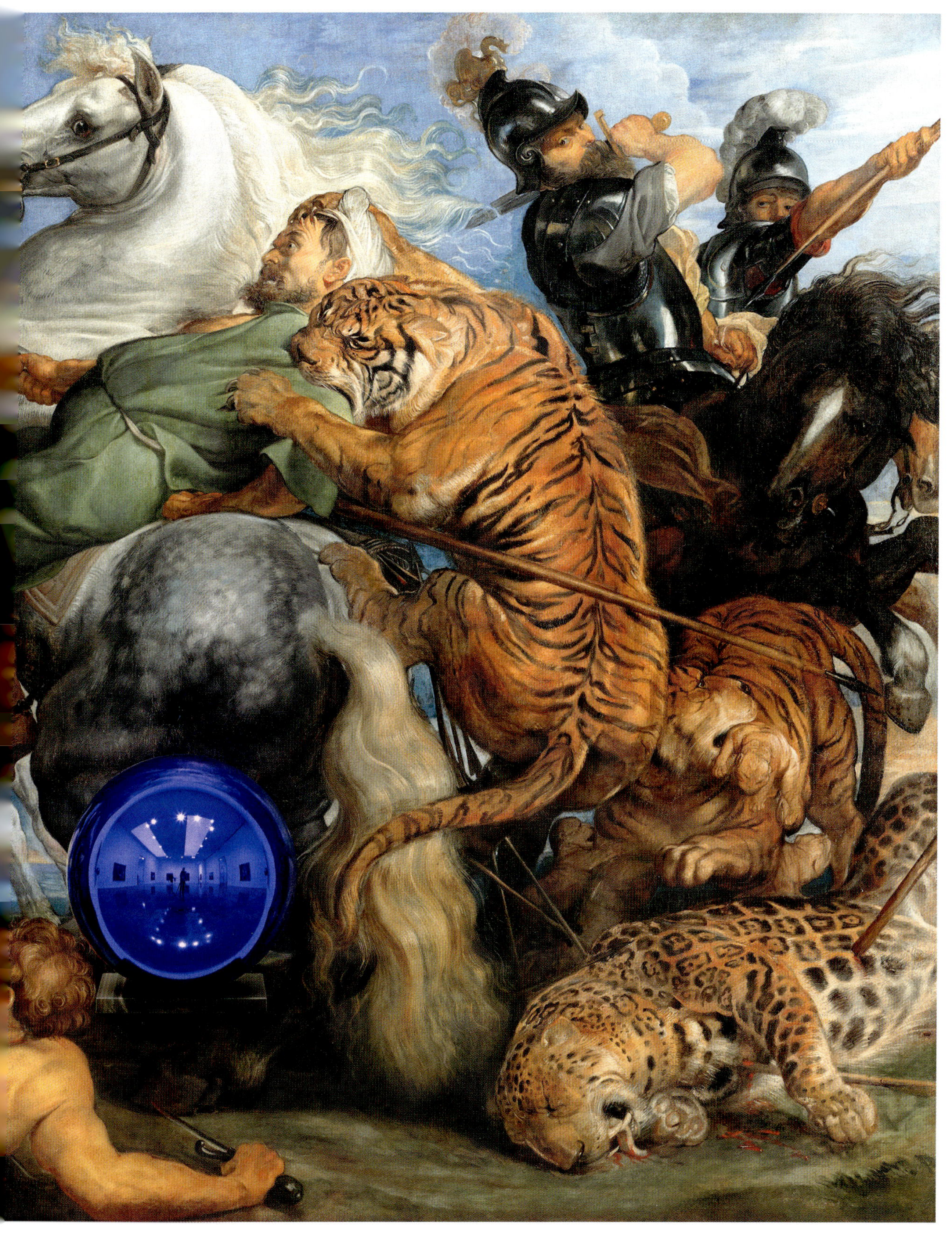

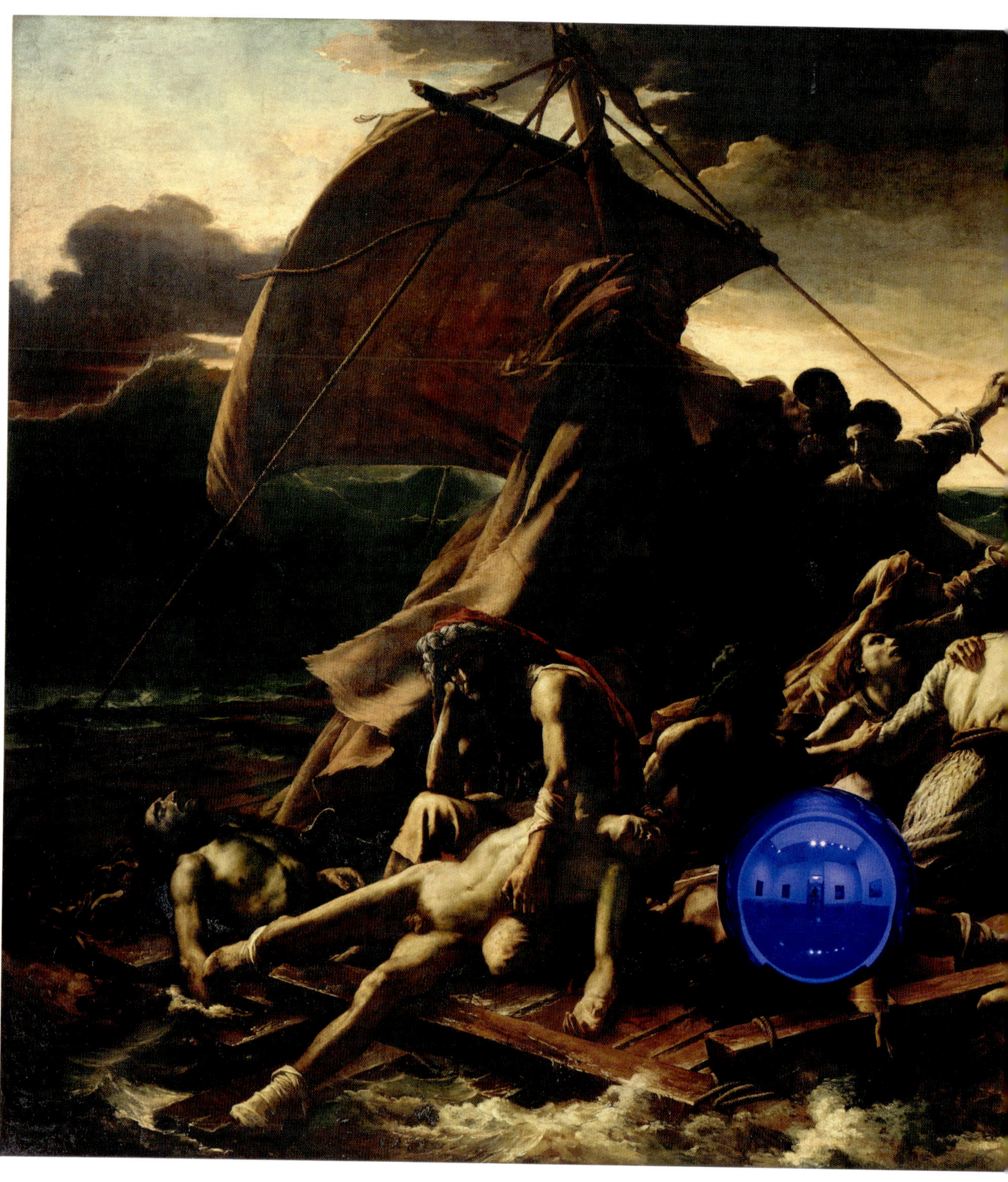

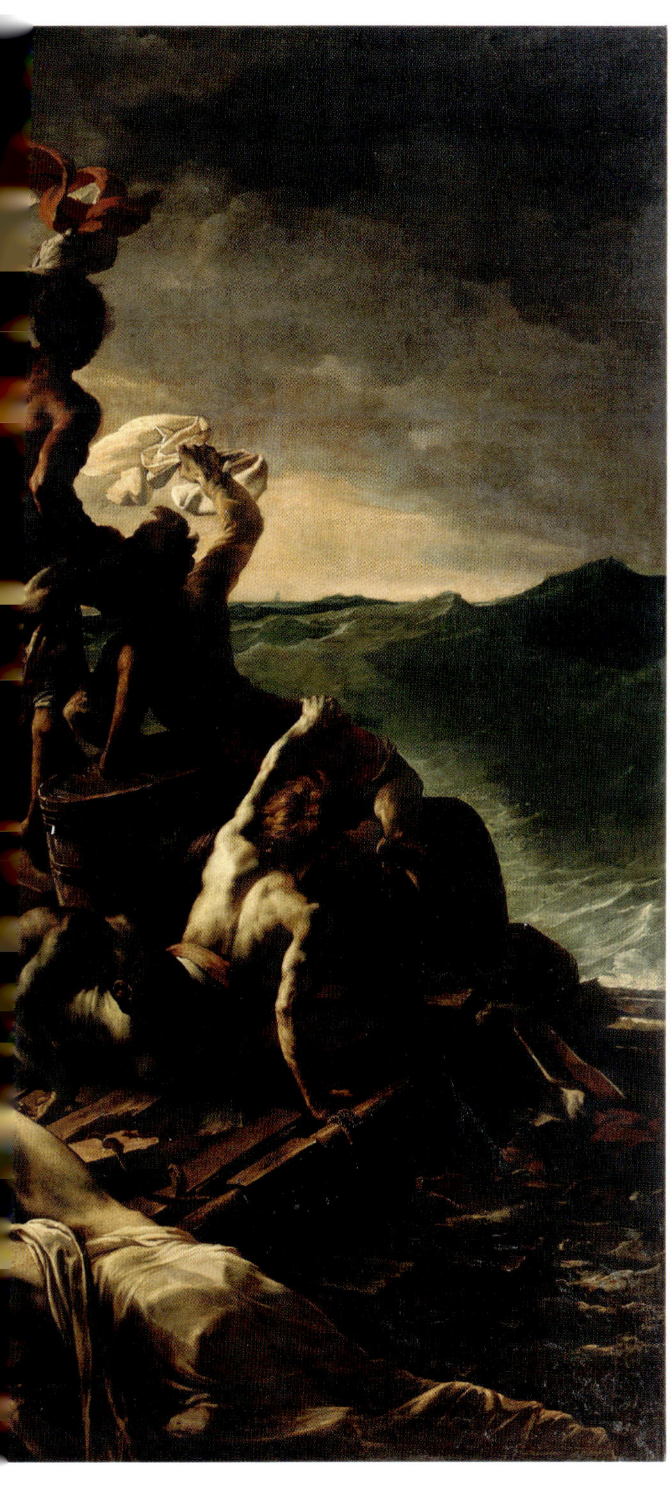

Gazing Ball (Géricault Raft of the Medusa)
Cat. 17

This experience is about you - your desires, your interests, your participation, your relationship with this image.

The *Raft of the Medusa*, painted in 1819 by Théodore Géricault (1791-1824), commemorates the abandonment of over 150 people on a makeshift raft after a ship called the *Medusa* sank, due to the captain's incompetence. All but a handful of them died, having resorted to murder and cannibalism.

The original painting is almost three times the size of this version. Appropriately for Koons, the work was revolutionary in its own day for using the huge scale normally reserved for biblical or historical subjects to show a distinctly unheroic subject. The painting has since become an icon of French Romanticism.

— 2014-15
— Oil on canvas, glass and aluminium
— 175.9 x 259 x 37.5 cm
— © Jeff Koons. Photo: Tom Powel Imaging. Courtesy Gagosian
— Collection of the artist

JEFF KOONS

Jeff Koons was born in York, Pennsylvania in 1955. He studied at the Maryland Institute College of Art in Baltimore and the School of the Art Institute of Chicago. He received a BFA from the Maryland Institute College of Art in 1976. Koons lives and works in New York City.

Since his first solo exhibition in 1980, Koons's work has been shown in major galleries and institutions throughout the world. His work was the subject of a major exhibition organised by the Whitney Museum of American Art, *Jeff Koons: A Retrospective* (27 June–19 October 2014), which travelled to the Centre Pompidou Paris (26 November 2014–27 April 2015) and the Guggenheim Bilbao (9 June–27 September 2015).

Koons is widely known for his iconic sculptures *Rabbit* and *Balloon Dog* as well as the monumental floral sculpture *Puppy* (1992), shown at Rockefeller Center and permanently installed at the Guggenheim Bilbao. Another floral sculpture, *Split-Rocker* (2000), previously installed at the Papal Palace in Avignon, Château de Versailles, Fondation Beyeler in Basel, Glenstone in Maryland and Rockefeller Center.

Jeff Koons has received numerous awards and honours in recognition of his cultural achievements. Notably, Koons received the Governor's Awards for the Arts 'Distinguished Arts Award' from the Pennsylvania Council on the Arts; the 'Golden Plate Award' from the Academy of Achievement; President Jacques Chirac promoted Koons to Officier de la Légion d'Honneur; and Secretary of State Hillary Rodham Clinton honoured Koons with the State Department's Medal of the Arts for his outstanding commitment to the Art in Embassies Program and international cultural exchange. In 2017, Koons was made the first Artist-in-Residence at Columbia University's Mortimer B. Zuckerman Mind Brain Behavior Institute and also made an Honorary Member of the University of Oxford's Edgar Wind Society for Outstanding Contribution for Visual Culture. Koons has been a board member of The International Centre for Missing & Exploited Children (ICMEC) since 2002. He co-founded the Koons Family International Law and Policy Institute with ICMEC for the purpose of combating global issues of child abduction and exploitation and to protect the world's children.

ACKNOWLEDGEMENTS

We are most grateful to all our lenders who are supporting our exhibition with objects:

The Broad Art Foundation
Stefan T. Edlis Collection
Collection of BZ + Michael Schwartz
Fundación Almine y Bernard Ruiz-Picasso para el Arte
Collectors who prefer to remain anonymous

Most of all we thank Jeff Koons and his studio for their generosity and support.